KETO

COOKBOOK FOR BEGINNERS

EASY LOW CARB, HIGH FAT RECIPES TO KICKSTART YOUR KETO LIFESTYLE

BY DEBBY HAYES

TABLE OF CONTENTS

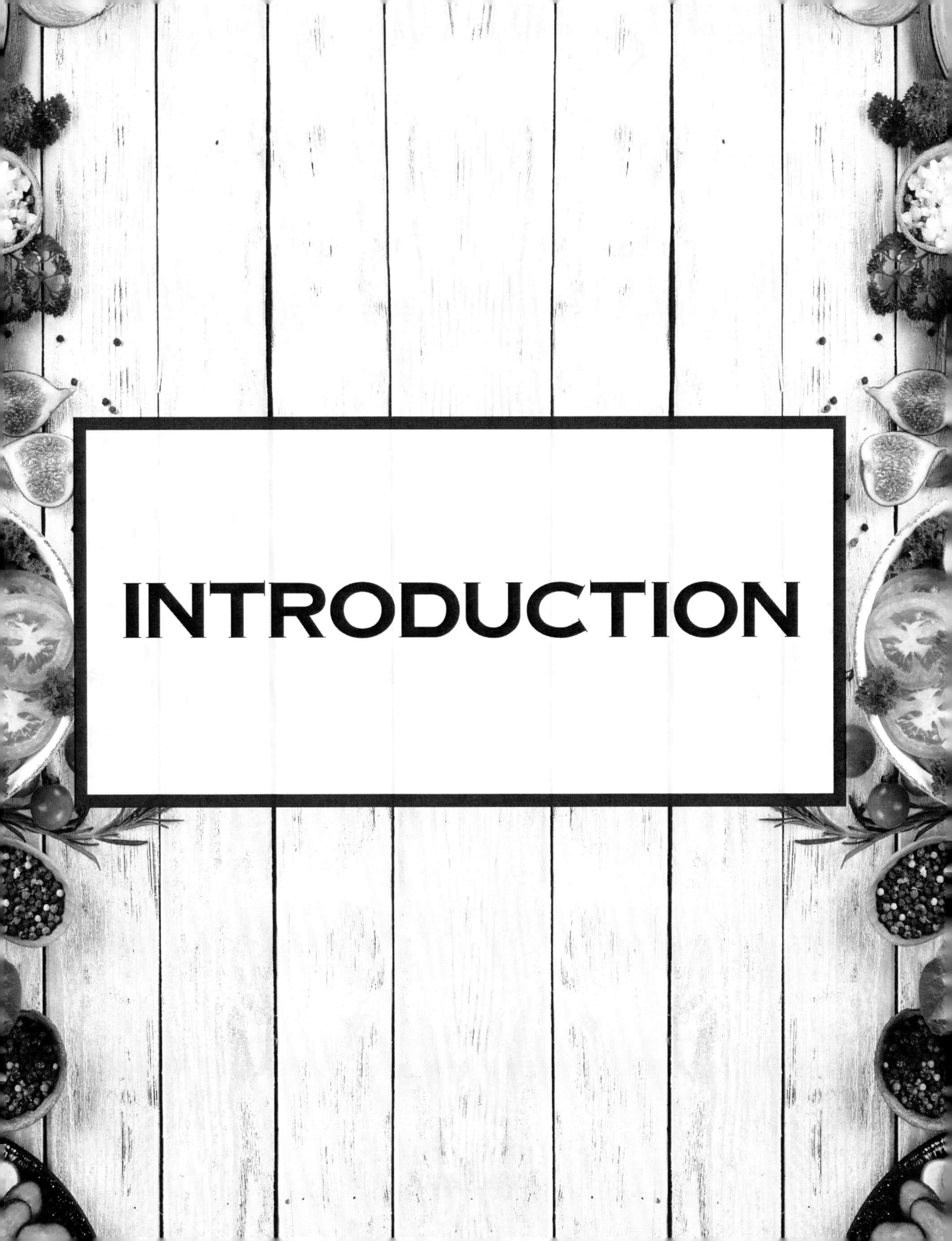

INTRODUCTION

The Ketogenic Diet has become a popular way for people to lose weight and gain health. Almost everyone you speak to has a story to share about their experience with this way of eating. The success stories tell of people losing fortunes of weight, reversing their Type 2 Diabetes, and increasing their energy levels. It must be worth a try!

The reason behind the success of the Ketogenic Diet is that it trains your body to stop relying on sugar for energy, and to start using fat as a fuel source instead. This means no more blood sugar spikes causing a rise in insulin levels. Too much sugar and insulin in the blood are the perfect recipe for weight gain and poor health.

The Ketogenic Diet is not a new concept, although it has only recently become popular amongst the general public. As far back as 500 BCE, physicians recognized that a diet high in fatty foods and low in starchy foods helped manage epilepsy. However, only in the 1920s did it become an important, recognized way to manage this condition in children. Medical professionals observed that the ketogenic diet mimicked the effects of fasting or starvation in the body. When the body is subjected to a severe lack of energy, chemicals called ketone bodies are released to replace that energy. The name of the diet comes from these chemicals. The process is called keto-genesis.

The first time The Ketogenic Diet was used for weight loss was in 1972, but it is only in the last ten to fifteen years that it has seen a surge in popularity. The diet is now a common topic for scientific research. There are studies that prove its effectiveness in managing weight and controlling disease, and as a result, we have a better understanding of why it is such a successful approach.

The most common nutrition advice is to eat a diet that provides 50% of your total daily calorie intake in the form of carbohydrates, 20% proteins, and 30% fats. The Ketogenic Diet contradicts these conventional recommendations. If you decide to follow The Ketogenic Diet, you will be advised to get 70% of your calories from fats, 20% from proteins, and only 10% from carbohydrates.

While the benefits of rapid weight loss and improved health are alluring, it can be difficult to figure out where to start with such a different way of eating. This diet has to be implemented correctly if you are to achieve ketosis, and all the health benefits that come with it. If you eat too many carbohydrates, you will not be able to achieve ketosis, and your body will not make the switch from glucose to fats for fuel.

As a dietitian, I have seen a lot of people who have tried The Ketogenic Diet, and failed, deciding it is not the diet for them. When I dig a little, it quickly becomes clear why they did not have the same results their best friend did. It is because they lacked an understanding of what carbohydrates are, and the effects they have on the body. Carbs and sugars sneak into your diet in surprising ways; some are more obvious than others. Perhaps the most common mistake I see people make is forgetting that the crumbs on their chicken schnitzel are made from bread. This is a definite no-no on The Ketogenic Diet.

With all that in mind, we have put together a collection of recipes to make The Ketogenic Diet easier for you to follow. Using quality, unprocessed ingredients in imaginative, tasty ways, you will soon be preparing meals that will become firm favorites in your household. Here, we have explained The Ketogenic Diet so that you understand why you are eating the way you are. We want your new diet to be implemented the right way, so that you achieve and maintain ketosis. That is how you will lose weight and feel more energized.

THE KETOGENIC DIET ABC

Let's start with the basics. The ketogenic diet is a low carbohydrate, high fat diet. It is recommended that you limit your carbohydrates to roughly 10% of your daily calorie intake, and increase your fat intake to 70%. If you are eating 2000 calories a day, that would equate to no more than 50 g of carbohydrates, and about 155 g of fat per day. Your proteins would account for roughly 20% of your daily calories, amounting to 100 g.

When you consider that the average 2000 calorie diet consists of 250 g of carbohydrates, 66 g of fats, and 100 g of protein, it is easy to understand where people might start going wrong. The idea that fats are bad for us has been firmly entrenched by decades of conventional "dietary wisdom". The ketogenic approach turns all that upside down.

It may seem a bit daunting, but don't close the book and give up before you start. Whether you are new to keto, or have been doing it for a while now, when you understand what the various kinds of foods do and are used for in your body, you will be able to make informed decisions about what to put on your plate.

MACRONUTRIENTS

Carbohydrates, fats, and proteins are called macronutrients, or macros. They all provide your body with energy in different ways:

- **Carbohydrates** from foods such as bread, potatoes, rice, and pasta are broken down in the digestive system to release glucose into the blood. Glucose is your body's preferred source of energy. It is absorbed rapidly from the digestive tract, and transported to the cells for energy.
- **Proteins** are not normally used for energy, except when there is an insufficient supply. If the body is deprived of glucose, protein will be broken down into ketone bodies that can then be used as fuel.
- **Fats** are a concentrated source of energy. They provide the body with twice as much energy per gram than both carbohydrates and proteins. Fat is digested slowly, and requires a significant amount of oxygen to convert it into ketone bodies that can be burned for energy. Because of the slow rate of digestion of fats, glucose will be used as fuel before fat is made available, if you are eating a conventional diet.

When you eat carbohydrate foods, they are broken down into glucose and released into the bloodstream, resulting in a rise in blood sugar levels. In response to this spike in blood sugar, insulin is released from the pancreas. Insulin unlocks the cells, allowing the sugar to move into the cells where it is used for energy. As a result, your blood sugar levels drop, and you get hungry again.

KETOSIS

When you eat refined carbohydrate foods and sugars, the time it takes for your blood sugar levels to spike and return to normal is a lot faster. The result is food cravings, particularly for more carbs, and greater hunger. Your body comes to rely on a very regular intake of glucose. The biggest problem with this blood sugar see-saw is that your body can only use a certain amount of energy at a time. That means that any excess glucose will be stored as fat, and you will gain weight.

When you restrict the amount of carbohydrates you eat, your body needs to find an alternative fuel source. On The Ketogenic Diet, that source is fat. When you limit your carbohydrate intake and eat more fats, your body is forced to use ketones for energy. The great thing about that is, not only are you burning ketones from dietary sources of fat, but you start using up your fat stores, as well.

It can take anywhere from a few days to a couple of weeks to reach this point. When you do, you are said to be in a state of ketosis. The amount of time it takes will depend on what you are eating, how much glycogen (sugar) you have stored in your body, and your activity level. If you restrict your carbohydrates to 10% of your daily intake, and get plenty of exercise, you will achieve ketosis much faster.

THE RIGHT WAY OR NOT AT ALL

So often we talk to people who say they are following The Ketogenic Diet, but then we see them eat a pizza for supper, or a gluten-free sandwich for lunch. They forget that the sugar in their tea, orange juice, or favorite soda also causes a blood sugar spike.

You will only benefit from the effects of The Ketogenic Diet if you achieve, and stay in, ketosis. As soon as any glucose from carbohydrates or sugars pushes your blood sugar levels up, your body says, "Thank you very much!", and starts using glucose for energy. Then you have to start the process all over again.

From my experience working with people who believe that The Ketogenic Diet is the answer they have been searching for in order to lose weight, it is usually a fear of fat that trips them up. We have been taught, over the last three decades, that fat is bad for us. So people attempt the keto diet without replacing their carbohydrate calories with fat calories. This leaves them feeling desperately hungry, and their sugar cravings ramp up to high gear.

Although fat is a calorie-dense macronutrient, it is what is going to help you lose weight. The only healthy way to achieve ketosis without starving yourself is by limiting your carbohydrate intake and increasing your fat intake. This is how your body learns to use fat for energy.

If you start feeling like you are coming down with something in the first week or two, don't give up. Feeling run down is normal in the beginning, while your body learns to prioritize fat for energy. You may experience symptoms like nausea, vomiting, constipation, diarrhea, headaches, moodiness, muscle weakness, and cramps. This is a temporary side effect of The Ketogenic Diet that may start in the first day or two after changing your way of eating. It normally lasts for less than a week.

THE BENEFITS OF A CLEAN KETOGENIC DIET

Clean eating refers to eating foods that are only minimally processed, or not at all. It means eating foods that have short ingredient lists. The aim is to minimize your intake of additives, colorants, artificial sweeteners, and preservatives. It also helps to reduce the amount of sugar and salt you eat.

Going back to basics, and cooking your food from scratch, makes it easier to follow The Ketogenic Diet, and it is better for your health. The benefits of a clean ketogenic diet include:

#1 Rapid Weight Loss

The primary purpose of The Ketogenic Diet is to encourage your body to burn fat for energy. When you achieve ketosis by following a clean ketogenic lifestyle, your body also benefits from the absence of the chemicals that are added to our food to increase flavor, enhance color, and lengthen shelf life. Many of these compounds can interfere with your metabolism and your hormones, and make it difficult for you to lose weight and stay healthy. So when you eliminate excessive carbohydrates, as well as all of these artificial chemicals, and enter ketosis, you will find yourself losing weight faster than you ever have before.

#2 Improved Energy Levels

Talk to anyone who has successfully implemented The Ketogenic Diet, and they will tell you that they are a lot more energetic than they were when they were eating a conventional diet. You probably won't feel this effect for the first few weeks, while your body makes the switch to burning fat, but once you get through the keto flu stage, your energy levels will start to climb. Your sugar cravings will become a thing of the past, and you will no longer have to deal with the dreaded afternoon energy slump when your blood sugar drops.

#3 Improved Cognitive Function

No more brain fog! When your brain is forced to start using ketones, particularly beta-hydroxybutyrate, for energy, it works better. You will benefit from improved mental clarity and enhanced cognitive function. Research has shown that ketones are a better source of fuel for the brain than glucose.

#4 Less Inflammation

Chronic inflammation is the driver for many health conditions, including type 2 diabetes, cardiovascular disease, obesity, autoimmune diseases, and dementia. High blood sugar levels have been linked to high levels of inflammation throughout the body. Therefore, when you control your blood sugar levels through The Ketogenic Diet, you are able to reduce the amount of inflammation in your body, improving your health. This effect is especially powerful when you eat foods that are free from additives, preservatives, and artificial sweeteners.

#5 Reduced Appetite

The Ketogenic Diet is a natural appetite suppressant. When you cut out carbohydrate foods, you automatically eat fewer calories without even trying. Unlike other diets, you will not feel hungry when you stick to The Ketogenic Diet.

WHAT CAN YOU EAT ON A KETOGENIC DIET?

Because you are training your body to burn fat instead of glucose for energy, you need to provide it with the appropriate fuel. That means strictly limiting your intake of carbohydrate foods, and significantly increasing your intake of fats.

Foods To Include In Your Clean Ketogenic Diet		
Fats	**Protein**	**Non-Starchy Vegetables**
Plant Oils:	Eggs	Spinach
Coconut oil	Beef	Lettuce
Avocado oil	Liver	Asparagus
Extra-virgin cold-pressed olive oil	Tripe	Cucumber
	Chicken	Zucchini
MCT oil	Turkey	Eggplant
	Pork	Tomato
Animal Fats:	Fish; especially dark, oily fish, such as salmon, trout, sardines, and mackerel	Kale
Butter		Cauliflower
Lard	Venison	Broccoli
Ghee	Lamb	Red, yellow, and green peppers
		Brussels sprouts
Fatty Foods:		Green beans
Avocado pears		Cabbage
Walnuts		Celery
Pistachio nuts		Onions
Cashew nuts		Garlic
Almonds		Leeks
Macadamia nuts		Radishes
Brazil nuts		Mushrooms
Pecan nuts		Swiss Chard
Olives		Snow peas
Coconut milk		Carrots
Nut and seed butters: sunflower seed, almond butter, macadamia nut butter		
Flaxseeds		
Chia seeds		

Fruit	Dairy	Other
Watermelon	Cheese	**Beverages:**
Strawberries	Heavy cream	Water
Lemons	Greek yogurt	Sparkling water
Raspberries		Bone broth
Blackberries		Coffee (unsweetened)
Cantaloupe		Tea (unsweetened)
Peaches		
Star fruit		**Seasoning:**
Plums		Salt
Fresh figs		Pepper
		Herbs (fresh and dried)
		Spices
		Lemon
		Lime
		Dijon mustard
		Vinegar

Foods To Avoid On Your Ketogenic Diet		
Grains	**Fruit**	**Starchy Vegetables**
All grains and grain products, including: Wheat Bread Corn Oats Rice Breakfast cereals Tortillas Wraps Bread rolls Barley	Bananas Grapes Dates Mangoes Pineapples Raisins Pears	**All starchy vegetables including:** Potatoes Sweet potatoes Butternut squash Beetroot Sweetcorn Peas
Sugars	**Beverages**	**Other**
White sugar Brown sugar Honey Maple syrup Syrup Agave High fructose corn syrup All artificial sweeteners	Beer Cider Sweet wine Sweet liquors Sodas Diet sodas Fruit juices Fruit-based smoothies Energy drinks	Refined oils, such as sunflower oil and canola oil Margarine Processed foods

10 TIPS FOR KETO SUCCESS

Whether you have been doing The Ketogenic Diet for a while, or whether it is a brand new adventure for you, being informed is the best way to begin, to ensure that you reap the rewards of this revolutionary style of eating. Knowing why you have to limit certain foods and focus on others makes it easier to make informed decisions about the foods you buy, prepare, and eat. Our recipes will make it easier for you to get started, ensuring you are eating a nutritionally complete diet that meets your body's needs.

Having a grocery list of foods is not enough to set you up for success. Eating is not as simple as buying the food and making it available in your kitchen. Your meals will require planning and preparation, and you may be faced with concepts and dilemmas you have never had to face in the kitchen before. So here are ten tips to make sure your ketogenic diet journey leads to weight loss and improved health.

1. Drink plenty of water every day. Aim for at least one and a half to two liters per day, and more if you are doing heavy exercise, and losing a lot of water through perspiration. Start your day with a big glass of water, and keep one handy throughout the day, so that it doesn't require any effort for you to do it.
2. Avoid artificial sweeteners. You may miss the sweetness of sugar when you first begin The Ketogenic Diet. Don't be tempted to replace sugar, honey, maple syrup, and all other forms of sugar with artificial sweeteners. They may not contain any calories, but your body may still believe it is getting sugar. This will make it much more difficult to achieve and sustain ketosis.
3. Be prepared for the "keto flu". Some people are lucky, and they don't experience any symptoms of the keto flu, but most will experience some effects of the body's transition from a glucose gobbler to a fat burning machine. The "flu" passes within a week, and then the real benefits begin to kick in.
4. Stock your pantry with ketogenic diet-friendly foods. If you are able to remove all foods that should be avoided on The Ketogenic Diet from your pantry, it will be easier to resist temptation. Make a shopping list, and make sure you have all the foods you need to prepare delicious, healthy, low-carb meals.
5. Do some meal preparation in advance; it always helps to be prepared. If you don't always have time at the end of the day to chop vegetables, spend some time over the weekend getting ready for the week to come. That way, all you have to do to prepare a healthy meal is cook the food.
6. Plan your macronutrient intake. Be aware of how much protein, carbohydrates, and fat you are consuming on a daily basis, to ensure that you stay in a ketogenic state.
7. Go for quality over quantity. This is especially true for protein foods. Try to buy grass-fed beef and free-range poultry. If this is out of your budget, buy the best quality food you can afford.
8. Have a plan for eating out. It isn't always easy to follow your ketogenic diet plan when you are not eating at home. As far as possible, avoid grains, starchy vegetables, and any processed sauces. Stick to grilled proteins, and vegetables or salad, wherever possible.
9. Know your low-carb swaps. There are low-carb foods you can swap for foods you would otherwise eat every day. For example, use butter instead of margarine, cold-pressed extra-virgin olive oil instead of sunflower oil, lettuce wraps in place of bread or flour tortillas.
10. Make the best food choices you can afford. It can be expensive to follow The Ketogenic Diet, especially when you are starting out. It may seem costly to "eat clean", but when you buy real food, rather than processed food, you will save money in the long run.

READY! SET! GO!

You are ready to dive into The Ketogenic Diet. It is a lifestyle change you won't regret. Cutting back on carbohydrates and eating more fat is a simple change to make that will result in rapid weight loss, improved energy levels, and better health. Dig in to our appetizing recipes that will have you looking forward to your next meal.

21 Day Meal Plan

B. Breakfast *L.* Lunch *D.* Dinner

DAY 1	DAY 2	DAY 3	DAY 4	DAY 5
B. Blueberry & Vanilla Smoothie Bowl ***L.*** Shrimp & Zucchini Noodles ***D.*** Oven Chicken Parmigiana	***B.*** Bacon Caramelized Onion Skillet ***L.*** Lettuce-Wrapped Chicken Sandwich ***D.*** Cheesy Burger Baked Casserole	***B.*** Corned Beef & Radish Hash ***L.*** Shrimp-Stuffed Avocados ***D.*** Quick & Easy Chicken Curry	***B.*** Eggy Ham & Salsa Cups ***L.*** Lamb & Mint Mini Meatloaves ***D.*** One-Pan Sea Bass Bake	***B.*** Keto-Friendly Waffles & Syrup ***L.*** Mediterranean Chicken Kebabs ***D.*** Simple Meatballs & Zucchini Noodles
DAY 6	**DAY 7**	**DAY 8**	**DAY 9**	**DAY 10**
B. Cheesy Scrambled Keto Eggs ***L.*** Cheesy Buffalo Chicken Salad ***D.*** Oven-Roasted Salmon & Bok Choy	***B.*** Keto-Friendly Waffles & Syrup ***L.*** Spicy Coriander Chicken Salad ***D.*** Sweet & Tangy Ginger Beef	***B.*** Eggy Ham & Salsa Cups ***L.*** Shrimp & Zucchini Noodles ***D.*** Three Cheese Buffalo Bake	***B.*** Cream Cheese & Salmon Eggs ***L.*** Cheesy Jalapeño & Sausage Bake ***D.*** Russian Pork Stew	***B.*** Spinach & Sausage Egg Pie ***L.*** Meaty Stuffed Bell Peppers ***D.*** Grilled, Curried Shrimp
DAY 11	**DAY 12**	**DAY 13**	**DAY 14**	**DAY 15**
B. One-Minute Lemon Breakfast Muffins ***L.*** Keto-Style Stir-Fry ***D.*** Spicy Mexican Chicken Rellenos	B. Corned Beef & Radish Hash ***L.*** Spicy Roasted Shrimp Salad ***D.*** Bangers & Creamy Cauliflower Mash	***B.*** Blueberry & Vanilla Smoothie Bowl ***L.*** Pork & Eggplant Roll-Ups ***D.*** Coconut Curry Broth with Mussels	***B.*** Spicy Baked Eggs ***L.*** French-Style Salmon Salad ***D.*** Keto-Friendly Baked Enchiladas	***B.*** Cheesy Scrambled Keto Eggs ***L.*** Hearts of Palm & Avo Salad ***D.*** Fiery Pork Vindaloo
DAY 16	**DAY 17**	**DAY 18**	**DAY 19**	**DAY 20**
B. Eggy Ham & Salsa Cups ***L.*** Nutty Chicken & Herb Salad ***D.*** Creamy Coconut Shrimp Stew	***B.*** Smoked Sausage & Eggs ***L.*** Mediterranean Chicken Kebabs ***D.*** Hard-Seared Rosemary Steaks	***B.*** Cream Cheese & Salmon Eggs ***L.*** Italian-Style Eggplant Bake ***D.*** Italian-Style Chicken & Zucchini Noodles	***B.*** Low-Carb Chocolate Coffee Muffins ***L.*** Simple Spicy Chicken Salad ***D.*** Chorizo & Spinach Soup	***B.*** Cauliflower-Crusted Sausage Skillet ***L.*** Easy Lemon & Butter Chicken ***D.*** Quick & Easy Oven Paella
DAY 21				
B. Keto-Friendly Waffles & Syrup ***L.*** Pork & Eggplant Roll-Ups ***D.*** Truffle Butter Pork Chops				

BREAKFASTS

BLUEBERRY & VANILLA SMOOTHIE BOWL

COOK TIME: 0 MINS | MAKES: 1 SERVING

INGREDIENTS:

- 2 tbsp. collagen peptides (aka hydrolysate)
- 1/3 cup fresh blueberries
- 1/2 cup chilled almond milk
- 1/2 tsp. pure vanilla essence
- 1 tbsp. shelled hemp seeds (hemp hearts)
- 3 tbsp. lightly toasted, unsweetened, shredded coconut

DIRECTIONS:

1. In a high-powered food processor, pulse the collagen powder, 2 tablespoons of blueberries, almond milk, and vanilla essence on high, until you have a lump-free mixture. Scrape the contents of the processor into a small serving bowl and refrigerate for 5 minutes, or just until the mixture has thickened to a yogurt-like consistency.

2. When the mixture is properly chilled, garnish with the rest of the blueberries, hemp seeds, and toasted coconut before serving. Serve immediately.

Per Serving:
Calories: 434, Fat: 35g, Protein: 14g, Carbohydrates: 14g, Fiber: 6g, Net Carbohydrates: 8g

CORNED BEEF & RADISH HASH

COOK TIME: 18 MINS | MAKES: 4 SERVINGS

INGREDIENTS:

- 1 tbsp. extra-virgin avocado oil
- 1/4 cup onions, diced
- 1 cup radishes, diced
- 1/2 tsp. Himalayan salt
- 1/4 tsp. freshly ground black pepper
- 1/4 tsp. garlic powder
- 1/2 tsp. crushed and dried oregano leaves
- 12 oz. canned corned beef

DIRECTIONS:

1. In a large frying pan over medium heat, heat the avocado oil. When the oil is nice and hot, fry the onions and radishes, along with the salt and pepper, for about 5 minutes, or just until the radishes are tender when pierced with a fork.

2. Stir in the garlic powder, oregano, and corned beef until all of the ingredients are properly combined. Reduce the heat to medium-low, and cook for 10 minutes, stirring at regular intervals to prevent burning.

3. When the radishes start to brown around the edges, firmly press the mixture into the bottom of the pan with a spatula or spoon. Bring the heat up to high, and cook for an additional 3 minutes, or until the bottom is a crispy golden brown.

4. Scrape the hash onto 4 plates, and serve hot.

Quick Tip:
Any leftovers can be refrigerated in an airtight container for no more than 5 days.

Per Serving:
Calories: 252, Fat: 16g, Protein: 23g, Carbohydrates: 3g, Fiber: 1g, Net Carbohydrates: 2g

EGGY HAM & SALSA CUPS

COOK TIME: 18 MINS | MAKES: 5 SERVINGS

INGREDIENTS:

- 8 large free-range eggs
- 1/3 cup store-bought salsa
- 1/2 tsp. Himalayan salt
- 1/4 tsp. freshly ground black pepper
- 1o slices deli ham
- 2 tbsp. fresh coriander leaves, chopped

DIRECTIONS:

1. Set the oven to preheat to 375°F, with the wire rack in the center of the oven.

2. In a medium-sized mixing bowl, whisk together the eggs, salsa, salt, and pepper, and set aside.

3. Use the ham to line 10 cups in a regular-sized muffin pan. Pour equal amounts of the egg and salsa mixture into the ham-lined cups.

4. Place the tray in the oven for 18 minutes, or until the eggs are no longer runny, and the edges are slightly browned.

5. Garnish the hot egg cups with fresh coriander leaves before serving.

Quick Tip:
Any leftovers can be refrigerated in an airtight container for no more than 5 days, or frozen for no more than 3 months. Reheat the cups in the microwave on high for 1-2 minutes until hot.

Per Serving:
Calories: 171, Fat: 9g, Protein: 20g, Carbohydrates: 2g, Fiber: 0g, Net Carbohydrates: 2g

CREAM CHEESE & SALMON EGGS

COOK TIME: 8 MINS | MAKES: 6 SERVINGS

INGREDIENTS:

- 2 tbsp. heavy cream
- 1/4 tsp. Himalayan salt
- 12 large free-range eggs
- 1 1/2 tbsp. butter
- 4 oz. smoked salmon, chopped into small pieces
- 3 tbsp. cream cheese
- 1 tbsp. fresh dill, chopped
- 1 tbsp. capers, rinsed and chopped
- 2 tbsp. red onions, finely chopped
- 2 lbs. heirloom tomatoes, sliced

DIRECTIONS:

1. Place the cream, salt, and eggs in a large mixing bowl, and use a fork to lightly beat the ingredients until everything is properly combined.

2. In a large frying pan over medium heat, melt the butter. When the butter is nice and hot, scrape the egg mixture into the pan, and fry for 6-8 minutes, stirring at regular intervals until the eggs are just about cooked. Stir in the salmon pieces and cream cheese for 1 additional minute, or until the eggs are properly cooked.

3. Scrape the cooked eggs onto a serving platter, and sprinkle the dill, capers, and red onions over the top in an even layer. Decorate the dish with sliced tomatoes before serving.

Per Serving:
Calories: 200, Fat: 16g, Protein: 16g, Carbohydrates: 2g, Fiber: 1g, Net Carbohydrates: 1g

CHEESY SCRAMBLED KETO EGGS

COOK TIME: 10 MINS | MAKES: 8 SERVINGS

INGREDIENTS:

- 14 large free-range eggs
- 1/2 tsp. Himalayan salt
- 1/4 tsp. freshly ground black pepper
- 3 tbsp. butter
- 6 oz. cream cheese
- 3 tbsp. spring onions, finely chopped

DIRECTIONS:

1. Whisk together the eggs, salt, and pepper in a large mixing bowl until properly combined.

2. Melt the butter in a large frying pan over medium heat. When the butter has melted, scrape the egg mixture into the pan, and cook for a few minutes until the eggs begin to set. Use a wooden spoon to gently scrape the eggs back and forth as they cook.

3. Add the cream cheese to the pan, and continue to stir until the cheese is incorporated and the eggs are properly cooked.

4. Scrape the eggs onto a serving platter, and garnish with the spring onions before serving hot.

Per Serving:
Calories: 245, Fat: 20g, Protein: 13g, Carbohydrates: 2g, Fiber: 0g, Net Carbohydrates: 2g

HOMEMADE KETO GRANOLA

COOK TIME: 45-50 MINS | MAKES: 10 SERVINGS

INGREDIENTS:

- 1/4 cup raw pumpkin seeds
- 1/2 cup raw walnuts, chopped
- 1/2 cup raw pecans, chopped
- 3/4 cup raw almond slivers
- 1 cup unsweetened coconut flakes
- 2 cups pork rinds, broken into small pieces
- 1/2 tsp. Himalayan salt
- 2 tbsp. ground cinnamon
- 2 tbsp. granulated sweetener
- 1 large egg white at room temperature
- 5 drops liquid sweetener
- 2 tsp. pure vanilla essence
- 1/3 cup melted coconut oil at room temperature

DIRECTIONS:

1. Set the oven to preheat to 250°F, with the wire rack in the center of the oven. Cover a large rimmed baking sheet with aluminum foil, and spray the foil with baking spray.

2. Place the pumpkin seeds, walnuts, pecans, almond slivers, coconut flakes, and pork rind pieces in a large mixing bowl, and toss to combine.

3. In a small glass bowl, mix together the salt, cinnamon, and granulated sweetener.

4. In a separate glass bowl, whisk the egg white until it resembles a fluffy, white cloud. Whisk in the liquid sweetener, vanilla, and coconut oil. Scrape the egg mixture into the bowl of nuts and pork rinds, tossing until all the ingredients are evenly coated. Sprinkle the spice mixture over everything in the bowl, and toss once more until all the ingredients are evenly coated with spice.

5. Scrape the granola onto the prepared baking sheet, and spread the mixture out in an even layer. Place the tray in the oven for 45-50 minutes, flipping and stirring the granola with a spatula every 15-20 minutes. When the granola is lightly toasted, switch off the oven, but don't remove the granola. Allow it to cool on the tray in the oven for 1-1 1/2 hours, with the door slightly open.

6. Serve the granola when it has cooled.

Per Serving:
Calories: 298, Fat: 32g, Protein: 12g, Carbohydrates: 5.9g, Fiber: 3.8g, Net Carbohydrates: 2.1g

ONE-MINUTE LEMON BREAKFAST MUFFINS

COOK TIME: 1 MIN | MAKES: 2 SERVING

INGREDIENTS:

- 1/2 tsp. baking powder
- 1 tbsp. coconut flour
- 2 tbsp. granulated sweetener
- 1/8 tsp. Himalayan salt
- 3 tbsp. blanched almond flour
- 1 tbsp. melted coconut oil at room temperature
- 2 tbsp. freshly squeezed lemon juice
- 1 large free-range egg, lightly beaten

DIRECTIONS:

1. Spray the insides of 2 large, microwave-safe coffee mugs with baking spray.

2. Place the baking powder, coconut flour, granulated sweetener, salt, and blanched almond flour in a large mixing bowl. Whisk the dry ingredients until everything is properly combined. Beat in the coconut oil, lemon juice, and egg until you have a lump-free batter.

3. Scrape the batter into the 2 prepared mugs in even amounts.

4. Place both mugs in the microwave on high for 1 minute, until set. If the batter is still too runny, continue to microwave the muffins on high for 20-second intervals, until set.

5. Use oven mitts to transfer the hot mugs to a wooden chopping board. Allow the muffins to cool for 5 minutes; they will become firmer as they cool.

6. Serve the muffins in the mugs with spoons, or gently loosen the edges with a sharp knife before turning them out onto a plate.

Quick Tip:
Any leftovers can be refrigerated in an airtight container for no more than 1 week.

Per Serving:
Calories: 222, Fat: 16.1g, Protein: 5.6g, Carbohydrates: 6.9g, Fiber: 4.2g, Net Carbohydrates: 2.7g

LOW-CARB CHOCOLATE COFFEE MUFFINS

COOK TIME: 20-22 MINS | MAKES: 12 SERVINGS

INGREDIENTS:

- 1/3 tsp. ground nutmeg
- 1/2 tsp. Himalayan salt
- 1 tsp. baking powder
- 2 tsp. instant coffee powder or espresso powder
- 1/2 cup unsweetened cocoa powder
- 1 2/3 cups blanched almond flour
- 3/4 cup granulated sweetener
- 1/4 cup softened cream cheese
- 1/2 cup softened unsalted butter
- 8 drops liquid sweetener
- 2 tsp. pure vanilla essence
- 1/4 cup heavy cream
- 1/3 cup melted refined coconut oil at room temperature
- 3 large free-range eggs

DIRECTIONS:

1. Set the oven to preheat to 350°F, with the wire rack in the center of the oven. Line a 12-cup muffin pan with cupcake holders.

2. Place the nutmeg, salt, baking powder, coffee, unsweetened cocoa powder, and almond flour in a medium-sized mixing bowl. Whisk the dry ingredients until everything is properly combined.

3. In a large mixing bowl, use a hand mixer to beat the granulated sweetener, cream cheese, and butter until you have a creamy mixture. Thoroughly beat in the liquid sweetener, vanilla, heavy cream, coconut oil, and eggs. Add the flour mixture to the bowl, and use a wooden spoon to combine the ingredients until you have a smooth batter.

4. Scrape the batter into the prepared muffin cups in even amounts; the batter should fill each cup about 2/3 of the way up. Place the muffin tin in the oven for 20-22 minutes, or until an inserted skewer comes out clean. Be careful not to overbake the muffins, as this will result in them becoming too dry, and crumbling.

5. Let the tray stand on the counter for 5 minutes before removing the muffins and serving.

Quick Tip:
Any leftovers can be refrigerated in an airtight container for no more than 1 week, or frozen for no more than 3 months.

Per Serving:
Calories: 178, Fat: 18.8g, Protein: 2.2g, Carbohydrates: 3.3g, Fiber: 1.6g, Net Carbohydrates: 1.7g

KETO-FRIENDLY WAFFLES & SYRUP

COOK TIME: 12 MINS | MAKES: 4 SERVINGS

INGREDIENTS:

For the waffles:

- 8 drops liquid sweetener
- 4 large free-range eggs
- 1 tsp. pure vanilla essence
- 1 tsp. baking powder
- 1/2 cup blanched almond flour
- 2 tbsp. coconut flour
- 1/4 cup granulated sweetener
- 1/4 cup softened cream cheese

For the Syrup:

- 5 1/2 tbsp. ghee
- 5 1/2 tbsp. powdered sweetener
- 2 tbsp. water (plus 2 tsp.)
- 3 drops liquid sweetener
- 1/8 tsp. Himalayan salt
- 1/3 tsp. ground nutmeg
- 3/4 tsp. pure maple essence
- 1 1/2 tsp. pure vanilla essence

DIRECTIONS:

1. Preheat the waffle iron on the lowest setting.

2. In a large mixing bowl, whisk together the liquid sweetener, eggs, vanilla, baking powder, almond flour, coconut flour, granulated sweetener, and cream cheese until you have a smooth batter.

3. When the waffle iron is hot, pour 1/2 cup of batter per waffle into the molds, and cook according to the waffle maker instructions, or until the waffles are golden. Use rubber-tipped tongs to remove the waffles once they are cooked; be careful, as the waffles will be slightly fragile until they've had time to cool. Repeat the process with the remaining batter. Set the waffles aside, and keep warm while you prepare the syrup.

4. In a small pot over low heat, melt the ghee. Add the powdered sweetener and water to the pot, whisking for 3-4 minutes while the syrup simmers.

5. Transfer the pot to a wooden chopping board, and whisk in the liquid sweetener, salt, nutmeg, maple essence, and vanilla essence. Whisk the syrup at regular intervals to prevent the sugars from crystallizing while it cools slightly.

6. Pour the warm syrup over the waffles, and serve immediately.

Quick Tip:

Any leftover waffles can be refrigerated in an airtight container for no more than 6 days, or frozen for no more than 2 months. The syrup is best served fresh.

Per Serving:

Calories: 158, Fat: 12.8g, Protein: 8.3g, Carbohydrates: 2.2g, Fiber: 0.4g, Net Carbohydrates: 1.8g

SMOKED SAUSAGE & EGGS

COOK TIME: 35 MINS | MAKES: 6 SERVINGS

INGREDIENTS:

- 1/4 cup heavy whipping cream
- 8 large free-range eggs
- 1 cup mozzarella cheese, grated
- Pinch of Himalayan salt
- Pinch of freshly ground black pepper
- 12 oz. smoked sausage, sliced
- 1/4 cup sliced spring onions (extra for garnish)
- 1 cup button mushrooms, diced

DIRECTIONS:

1. Whisk together the cream and eggs in a medium-sized mixing bowl. Fold in the cheese, and a pinch each of salt and pepper. Let the egg mixture stand on the counter while you prepare the rest of the dish.

2. Set the oven to preheat to 400°F, with the wire rack in the center of the oven.

3. Heat a non-stick, oven-safe frying pan over medium heat before adding the sausage, and frying for 5-6 minutes or until evenly browned. Add the spring onions and mushrooms to the pan, and stir for an additional 5 minutes, or until the mushrooms darken in color. Turn off the heat.

4. Carefully pour the cheesy egg mixture over all of the ingredients in the pan. Place the pan in the oven, and bake for 25 minutes or until the eggs are no longer runny.

5. Gently loosen the edges of the egg around the pan with a sharp knife before slicing. Serve the eggs and sausage hot, garnished with extra spring onions.

Quick Tip:
Any leftovers can be refrigerated in an airtight container for no more than 5 days. Reheat the leftovers in the microwave just until warm; overheating will result in the eggs becoming rubbery.

Per Serving:
Calories: 281, Fat: 22.6g, Protein: 15.9g, Carbohydrates: 2.6g, Fiber: 0.2g, Net Carbohydrates: 2.4g

CAULIFLOWER-CRUSTED SAUSAGE SKILLET

COOK TIME: 42 MINS | MAKES: 8 SERVINGS

INGREDIENTS:

- 1 tsp. extra-virgin olive oil
- 12 oz. frozen riced cauliflower
- 1/2 tsp. Himalayan salt (divided)
- 1/2 cup parmesan cheese, grated
- 7 large free-range eggs (divided)
- 1 tsp. extra-virgin avocado oil
- 2 tbsp. spring onions, chopped
- 1/2 cup red bell peppers, diced
- 6 slices bacon, chopped
- 8 oz. bulk breakfast sausage
- 1/2 tsp. freshly ground black pepper

DIRECTIONS:

1. Set the oven to preheat to 425°F, with the wire rack in the center of the oven. Grease a large, oven-safe frying pan with 1 teaspoon of olive oil.

2. Prepare the riced cauliflower by following the directions on the packaging. When the cauliflower is cooked, allow it to cool, and use a clean kitchen towel or cheesecloth to press out any excess water. Place the drained cauliflower in a large mixing bowl, and add 1/4 teaspoon of salt, all of the parmesan cheese, and 1 large free-range egg. Mix the ingredients until everything is properly combined.

3. Spoon the cauliflower mixture into the oiled pan, and use a wooden spoon or the back of a clean glass to press the mixture into the pan and form a crust. Be sure to get some of the cauliflower pressed up the edges of the pan, as well.

4. Prebake the crust in the oven for 12 minutes, or until the edges are nicely browned. Allow the crust to cool in the pan on the counter while you prepare the rest of the dish. Don't switch the oven off at this point, as you will still need to bake the filling.

5. In a clean frying pan, heat the avocado oil over medium heat. When the oil is nice and hot, fry the spring onions, bell peppers, bacon, and sausage for about 10 minutes, or until all of the meat is properly cooked. Use a wooden spoon to break up the sausage into smaller pieces as it cooks. Once the meat is done, transfer the pan to a wooden chopping board, and set aside.

6. In a medium-sized mixing bowl, beat the remaining eggs and salt together, along with the black pepper. Scrape the slightly cooled sausage mixture into the bowl of eggs, and stir until all of the ingredients are properly combined. Pour the mixture into the cooled cauliflower crust.

7. Place the pan in the oven for 20 minutes, or until the eggs are no longer runny; they should be firm to the touch.

8. Use a sharp knife to gently pry the crust away from the edges of the pan, before slicing and serving hot.

Per Serving:
Calories: 338, Fat: 26g, Protein: 19.7g, Carbohydrates: 5.8g, Fiber: 2.5g, Net Carbohydrates: 3.3g

SPINACH & SAUSAGE EGG PIE

COOK TIME: 40 MINS | MAKES: 6 SERVINGS

INGREDIENTS:

- 1/2 cup grated pecorino cheese
- 1/4 tsp. Himalayan salt
- 1/2 tsp. freshly ground black pepper
- 1/2 cup whole milk
- 12 large free-range eggs
- 2 tbsp. extra-virgin avocado oil
- 1 small onion, finely chopped
- 1/2 lb. Italian sausage, casings removed
- 3 cups chopped spinach leaves, stems removed
- 1 cup no-sugar-added marinara sauce
- 6 oz. fresh mozzarella cheese, sliced
- Fresh basil leaves for garnish

DIRECTIONS:

1. Set the oven to preheat to 350°F, with the wire rack in the center of the oven.

2. Place the pecorino cheese, salt, pepper, whole milk, and eggs in a large mixing bowl, and whisk until all of the ingredients are properly combined. Set aside.

3. Heat the avocado oil in a large, oven-safe frying pan over medium heat. When the oil is nice and hot, fry the onions for about 5 minutes, or until they become translucent. Stir in the sausage for 5 minutes, until all of the pieces are properly cooked. Use a wooden spoon to break the sausage apart as it cooks. Stir in the spinach leaves for 1 additional minute, or until the leaves reduce in size.

4. Carefully pour the egg mixture into the pan after lowering the heat. Stir until the egg mixture is properly incorporated.

5. Transfer the pan to the oven for 18-20 minutes, until the eggs are no longer runny, but not cooked all the way through. Remove the pan from the oven and preheat the broiler.

6. Use an offset spatula or the back of a wooden spoon to carefully spread the marinara sauce over the top of the egg pie. Layer the mozzarella evenly over the sauce, and return the pan to the oven for 5 minutes, until the cheese is bubbling and lightly toasted.

7. Garnish the pie with the fresh basil leaves before slicing and serving warm.

Quick Tip:
Any leftovers can be refrigerated in an airtight container for no more than 3 days.

Per Serving:
Calories: 480, Fat: 37g, Protein: 28g, Carbohydrates: 8g, Fiber: 2g, Net Carbohydrates: 6g

BACON CARAMELIZED ONION SKILLET

COOK TIME: 35 MINS | MAKES: 9 SERVINGS

INGREDIENTS:

- 6 slices thick-cut bacon, cut into small cubes
- 1/2 cup onions, chopped
- 1/2 tsp. Himalayan salt
- 1/4 tsp. freshly ground black pepper
- 1/4 cup almond milk
- 10 large free-range eggs
- 1 tbsp. fresh parsley, chopped (for garnish)

DIRECTIONS:

1. Set the oven to preheat to 375°F, with the wire rack in the center of the oven.

2. In a large, oven-safe frying pan over medium heat, fry the bacon and onions, along with the salt and pepper, for about 10 minutes, or until the bacon is nice and crispy, and the onions begin to caramelize. Stir at regular intervals to prevent burning. When the bacon and onions are done, transfer the pan to a wooden chopping board, and allow to cool slightly.

3. In a large mixing bowl, whisk together the almond milk and eggs, until the mixture is light and frothy.

4. Once the pan has cooled slightly, carefully pour the eggs and almond milk over everything in the pan, taking care not to move the bacon and onions.

5. Place the pan in the oven for 25 minutes, or until the eggs are properly cooked and firm to the touch.

6. Allow the pan to stand for 5 minutes on the counter before slicing. Serve garnished with parsley.

Quick Tip:
Any leftovers can be refrigerated in an airtight container for no more than 5 days, or frozen for no more than 3 months.

Per Serving:
Calories: 146, Fat: 9g, Protein: 11g, Carbohydrates: 1g, Fiber: 0g, Net Carbohydrates: 1g

SPICY BAKED EGGS

COOK TIME: 35 MINS | MAKES: 5 SERVINGS

INGREDIENTS:

- 1 lb. Mexican-style chorizo sausage, casings removed, chopped
- 1 tsp. ground cumin
- 1 tsp. crushed garlic
- 1/3 cup onions, chopped
- 1/2 cup poblano peppers, chopped
- 1/2 tsp. Himalayan salt
- 1/4 tsp. freshly ground black pepper
- 1 cup canned crushed tomatoes
- 5 large free range eggs
- 2 tbsp. fresh coriander leaves, chopped (for garnish)

DIRECTIONS:

1. Set the oven to preheat to 375°F, with the wire rack in the center of the oven.

2. In a large, oven-safe frying pan over medium heat, fry the chopped chorizo for about 5 minutes, breaking the sausage apart with a wooden spoon as it cooks. Stir in the cumin, garlic, onions, poblano peppers, salt, and pepper for an additional 5 minutes, or until the onions become translucent. Stir in the tomatoes, and allow the mixture to simmer for 5 minutes while stirring, until the sauce reduces slightly.

3. Transfer the pan to a wooden chopping board, and use a wooden spoon to create 5 small pockets in the sauce. Carefully crack each egg into its own pocket, taking care not to break the yolks.

4. Place the pan in the oven for 15-20 minutes, or until the egg whites are hard, and the yolks are cooked to the desired level. Remove the pan from the oven after 15 minutes if you prefer runny yolks.

5. Sprinkle the coriander leaves over everything in the dish before serving hot.

Quick Tip: Any leftovers can be refrigerated in an airtight container for no more than 5 days.

Per Serving:
Calories: 343, Fat: 28g, Protein: 19g, Carbohydrates: 8g, Fiber: 2g, Net Carbohydrates: 6g

SNACKS

CRUSTLESS SKILLET PIZZA

COOK TIME: 10-20 MINS | MAKES: 3 SERVINGS

INGREDIENTS:

For the marinara sauce:

- 1/4 tsp. Himalayan salt
- 1/4 tsp. freshly ground black pepper
- 1/4 cup extra-virgin olive oil
- 1/4 cup tomato paste
- 1 small white onion, chopped
- 2 whole garlic cloves
- 1/2 cup fresh basil leaves
- 1 cup tomatoes, chopped

Pizza:

- 1 tbsp. ghee
- 1 small yellow onion, chopped
- 4 oz. fresh kale, stems removed, chopped
- 6 large free-range eggs
- 1 cup mozzarella cheese, grated (divided)
- 1/3 cup parmesan cheese, grated (divided)
- 1/4 cup kalamata olives, halved
- 2 medium heirloom tomatoes, sliced
- 1 tbsp. extra-virgin avocado oil
- Fresh basil leaves for garnish

DIRECTIONS:

1. In a high-powered food processor, blend the salt, pepper, olive oil, tomato paste, onion, garlic, basil leaves, and tomatoes on high, until you have a smooth sauce. Scrape the marinara sauce into a bowl, and set aside while you prepare the pizza.

2. Melt the ghee in a large, oven-safe frying pan over medium-high heat, swirling the pan to coat the sides and bottom. When the ghee is nice and hot, fry the onions for 3 minutes, or until fragrant.

3. Stir in the kale for 1 minute. If all of the kale does not fit comfortably in the pan, allow some of it to cook down before adding more.

4. Set the oven broiler to preheat on high.

5. In a large bowl, beat the eggs until frothy. Add half of the mozzarella and half of the parmesan to the eggs, and beat again. Remove 1/3 cup of the marinara sauce, and refrigerate the remainder in an airtight container for no more than 5 days. Add half of the 1/3 cup of marinara to the eggs, and beat until all of the ingredients are properly combined.

6. Carefully pour the egg mixture into the pan of cooked onions, and cook for 8-10 minutes over medium-low with a lid on the pan, or just until the eggs are no longer runny, but not completely cooked.

7. Transfer the pan to a wooden chopping board. Pour the remaining marinara sauce from the 1/3 cup over the top, followed by the remaining mozzarella and parmesan. Garnish the pizza with the olives and tomatoes slices.

8. Place the pan under the broiler for 5-7 minutes, or until the cheese bubbles and becomes a crispy, golden brown.

9. Allow the pizza to cool for 5 minutes on the counter before garnishing with the basil leaves and avocado oil. Slice the pizza, and serve hot.

Per Serving:

Calories: 473, Fat: 34.9g, Protein: 28.1g, Carbohydrates: 9.6g, Fiber: 2.5g, Net Carbohydrates: 7.1g

SMOKED SALMON & PISTACHIO NUGGETS

COOK TIME: 0 MINS | MAKES: 12 SERVINGS

INGREDIENTS:

- 1/2 tsp. ground ginger
- 1 tsp. toasted sesame oil
- 2 tsp. freshly squeezed lime juice
- 1/2 tsp. finely grated lime zest
- 1/4 cup butter, room temperature
- 4 oz. cream cheese, room temperature
- 2 oz. smoked salmon, chopped
- 3 tbsp. lightly toasted pistachios, chopped

DIRECTIONS:

1. Cover a large, rimmed baking tray with grease-proof paper, and set aside.

2. Add the ginger, toasted sesame oil, lime juice, lime zest, butter, and cream cheese to a large mixing bowl. Use a wooden spoon to stir the ingredients until everything is properly combined. Gently fold in the smoked salmon.

3. Divide the mixture into 12 nuggets of roughly the same size, and space them evenly on the prepared baking tray.

4. Chill the tray for 1-2 hours, until the nuggets are firm to the touch.

5. Place the chopped pistachios in a shallow dish, and quickly roll each nugget in the nuts. Place the coated nuggets on a serving platter, and garnish with the remaining pistachios before serving.

Quick Tip:
Any leftovers can be refrigerated in an airtight container for no more than 1 week.

Per Serving:
Calories: 85, Fat: 9g, Protein: 2g, Carbohydrates: 1g, Fiber: 0g, Net Carbohydrates: 1g

CHILLED CHEESY PIZZA TOSS

COOK TIME: 0 MINS | MAKES: 8 SERVINGS

INGREDIENTS:

- 1/4 tsp. Italian seasoning
- 1/2 tsp. dried basil
- 2 tbsp. balsamic vinegar
- 3 tbsp. extra-virgin olive oil
- 1 tbsp. Kalamata olives, halved
- 2 tbsp. onions, finely chopped
- 2 tbsp. sun-dried tomatoes in oil, finely chopped
- 1/3 cup roasted red peppers, finely chopped
- 4 oz. pepperoni, chopped
- 8 oz. feta cheese, crumbled
- Fresh basil leaves for garnish

DIRECTIONS:

1. In a large mixing bowl, toss the Italian seasoning, dried basil, balsamic vinegar, olive oil, olives, onions, sun-dried tomatoes, roasted red peppers, pepperoni, and feta, until all of the ingredients are properly combined.

2. Cover, and refrigerate the bowl for at least 1 hour.

3. Garnish the bowl with fresh basil leaves before serving.

Quick Tip:
Any leftovers can be refrigerated for no more than 5 days in an airtight container.

Per Serving:
Calories: 330, Fat: 24.4g, Protein: 22.9g, Carbohydrates: 4.9g, Fiber: 1g, Net Carbohydrates: 3.9g

SPICY LIME-BAKED TRAIL MIX

COOK TIME: 1-1 1/2 HOURS | MAKES: 5-6 SERVINGS

INGREDIENTS:

- 1/2 tsp. onion powder
- 1/2 tsp. garlic powder
- 1/2 tsp. crushed red pepper flakes
- 2 tsp. Himalayan salt
- 3 tbsp. chili powder
- 1/4 cup raw pumpkin seeds
- 1/2 cup raw pecans, roughly chopped
- 1/2 cup raw cashews, roughly chopped
- 1/4 cup raw almond slivers
- 1 cup raw peanuts
- 3 cups pork rind pieces, chopped
- 3 cups parmesan cheese crisps, broken into small pieces
- 1 large free-range egg white
- 3 1/2 tbsp. freshly squeezed lime juice

DIRECTIONS:

1. Line a large, rimmed baking tray with aluminum foil. Lightly coat the foil with baking spray, and set the oven to preheat to 200°F, with the wire rack in the center of the oven.

2. In a small bowl, mix together the onion powder, garlic powder, crushed red pepper flakes, salt, and chili powder. Set aside. In a large bowl, toss together the pumpkin seeds, pecans, cashews, almond slivers, peanuts, pork rinds, and parmesan cheese crisps, until everything is properly combined.

3. Place the egg white in a small glass bowl, and whisk until frothy. Add in the lime juice, and whisk until the mixture is light and frothy, and the juice is properly incorporated into the egg white.

4. Scrape the egg white and lime juice into the bowl of mixed nuts and pork rinds. Toss until all of the ingredients are evenly coated in the egg mixture. Sprinkle the spices over everything in the bowl, and toss once more until the spices are evenly distributed.

5. Scrape the mixture onto the prepared baking tray in an even layer. Bake in the oven for about 1 1/2 hours, or until the nuts are a crispy, golden brown. Use a spatula to turn and stir the nuts every 15-20 minutes, to ensure even roasting. When the nuts are all evenly roasted, turn the oven off with the trail mix inside, and leave the door ajar with the light on for 1-1 1/2 hours, allowing the heat to escape, and the mix to become crispier.

6. Allow the mix to cool in the tray on the counter for a few minutes before serving.

Quick Tip:
Any leftovers can be refrigerated in an airtight container for no more than 2 weeks.

Per Serving:
Calories: 298, Fat: 28.2g, Protein: 26g, Carbohydrates: 6.4g, Fiber: 3.1g, Net Carbohydrates: 3.3g

BEEFY HORSERADISH SAUCE BITES

COOK TIME: 1 1/2 HOURS | MAKES: 16 SERVINGS

INGREDIENTS:

- 1/4 cup heavy whipping cream
- 1/4 tsp. Himalayan salt
- 1/4 tsp. freshly ground black pepper
- 2 tsp. whole-grain French mustard
- 2 tsp. freshly squeezed lime juice
- 3 tbsp. prepared horseradish
- 2 tbsp. avocado oil mayonnaise
- 2 tbsp. full-fat sour cream
- 16 thin slices roast beef
- 32 dill pickle slices

DIRECTIONS:

1. Use a handheld blender to beat the cream until it just starts to thicken; about 30-45 seconds on the highest setting.

2. Place the salt, pepper, mustard, lime juice, horseradish, mayonnaise, and sour cream in a large mixing bowl, and stir until all of the ingredients are properly combined. Gently fold in the whipped cream until everything is properly incorporated. Cover, and chill the bowl for up to 24 hours, or until ready to use.

3. Cut the roast beef slices down to roughly the same size as the pickle slices, or until you have 32 pieces. Divide the pickle and beef slices between 16 skewers; 2 slices of beef and 2 slices of pickle per skewer. Build the skewers by alternating between the beef and pickle slices.

4. Serve the skewers on a platter, with the chilled sauce drizzled over all the skewers, or on the side for dipping.

Per Serving:
Calories: 160, Fat: 13g, Protein: 7g, Carbohydrates: 4g, Fiber 0.3g, Net Carbohydrates: 3.7g

SOUR CREAM CHEESE BITES

COOK TIME: 0 MINS | MAKES: 5 SERVINGS

INGREDIENTS:

- 1 tsp. onion powder
- 1 tsp. garlic powder
- 1/4 tsp. Himalayan salt
- 1/4 tsp. freshly ground black pepper
- 1 tsp. prepared horseradish
- 1/2 cup grated mozzarella cheese
- 1/4 cup full-fat sour cream
- 4 oz. cream cheese, at room temperature
- 1/2 cup toasted sesame seeds

DIRECTIONS:

1. In a large mixing bowl, use a handheld mixer to beat the onion powder, garlic powder, salt, pepper, horseradish, mozzarella, sour cream, and cream cheese on high for about 1 minute, until you have a smooth mixture. Cover the bowl, and chill for 10-15 minutes.

2. Using clean hands, divide the mixture into 20 balls of roughly the same size. Place the sesame seeds in a shallow bowl, and roll each ball in the seeds before placing it on a serving platter. Chill the balls until ready to serve.

Per Serving:
Calories: 225, Fat: 21g, Protein: 8g, Carbohydrates: 6g, Fiber 2g, Net Carbohydrates: 4g

COCONUT LEMON BITES

COOK TIME: 1 MIN | MAKES: 10 SERVINGS

INGREDIENTS:

- 2 tbsp. coconut butter
- 1/4 cup coconut oil
- 1 cup lightly toasted macadamia nuts
- 1/4 tsp. Himalayan salt
- 2 tbsp. freshly squeezed lemon juice
- 1/2 tsp. pure vanilla essence
- 2 scoops vanilla flavored whey protein powder
- 1/3 cup unsweetened shredded coconut

DIRECTIONS:

1. Melt the coconut butter and coconut oil in a microwave-safe bowl on high for 25 seconds. Use a fork to beat the 2 ingredients together before setting the bowl aside on the counter.

2. Pulse the macadamia nuts on high in a high-powered blender for 30 seconds. Push the nuts down, and add the salt, lemon juice, and vanilla, along with the coconut mixture. Pulse the mixture until you have a lump-free paste. Add the protein powder, and pulse a few times until the powder is just incorporated into the mixture.

3. Scrape the batter into a small glass bowl. Cover the bowl with cling wrap, and chill for 15 minutes, or until the mixture is no longer runny, and has become easy to work with.

4. Line a rimmed baking sheet with grease-proof paper. Working with clean hands, form the firmed batter into 20 balls of roughly the same size, and place them on the prepared baking sheet.

5. Place the shredded coconut in a shallow bowl. Roll each ball in the coconut before returning it to the sheet. Once all of the balls are coated in coconut, place the sheet in the freezer for 30 minutes, or until the balls have hardened.

6. Allow the sheet to sit at room temperature for about 5 minutes before serving.

Quick Tip:
Any leftovers should be returned to the freezer and stored in an airtight container, as this recipe tends to melt quickly.

Per Serving:
Calories: 182, Fat: 17g, Protein: 5g, Carbohydrates: 4g, Fiber: 1.2g, Net Carbohydrates: 2.8g

SOUTHERN-THEMED BBQ PIZZA

COOK TIME: 30 MINS | MAKES: 4 SERVINGS

INGREDIENTS:

- 1/4 cup cream cheese
- 2 cups mozzarella cheese, grated
- 1 tsp. garlic powder
- 2 tsp. baking powder
- 3/4 cup finely ground, blanched almond flour
- 1 large free-range egg
- 1/2 cup store-bought BBQ sauce (extra for serving)
- 1 cup shredded pulled pork, store-bought or homemade
- 1 cup cheddar cheese, grated
- 2 miniature bell peppers, thinly sliced

DIRECTIONS:

1. Set the oven to preheat to 425°F, with the wire rack in the center of the oven.

2. Place the cream cheese and mozzarella in a large glass bowl, and microwave on high, stirring every 30 seconds for about 90 seconds. Stir the cheese until you have a lump-free paste, and the 2 cheeses are properly combined.

3. Stir in the garlic powder, baking powder, almond flour, and egg until the ingredients just come together. Return the bowl to the microwave for an additional 10 seconds. Use clean hands to properly combine all of the ingredients, and bring the dough together in a smooth ball. If the dough is too sticky to work with, use a small amount of olive oil on your hands to make the process easier. Cover the dough in cling wrap, and chill for 10 minutes.

4. Once the dough has chilled, roll it out into the desired shape between 2 sheets of greaseproof paper. Your base should be about 1/4-inch thick.

5. Discard the top sheet of grease-proof paper, and transfer the rolled-out dough, still on the bottom piece of paper, to a baking pan. Poke holes all over the crust with a fork before baking it in the oven for 10 minutes. Check the crust to see if any bubbles have formed, and if they have, use a fork to pop them before returning the crust to the oven for 5-8 minutes, or until lightly toasted.

6. Spread the BBQ sauce over the base in an even layer, followed by the pulled pork and cheddar cheese. Arrange the bell peppers on top.

7. Return the pizza to the oven for an additional 10 minutes, or until the cheese is bubbling and lightly browned. Slice the pizza, and serve hot with extra BBQ sauce if desired.

Per Serving:
Calories: 274, Fat: 19.8g, Protein: 16.5g, Carbohydrates: 6.6g, Fiber 1.8g, Net Carbohydrates: 4.8g

CHEESY, ITALIAN-STUFFED PEPPERS

COOK TIME: 25 MINS | MAKES: 4 SERVINGS

INGREDIENTS:

- 1 lb. chorizo sausage, casings removed
- 1 cup marinara sauce
- 4 large sweet peppers, any color
- Italian seasoning for sprinkling
- 1 cup mozzarella cheese, grated
- 16 pepperoni slices
- Parmesan cheese, grated (for garnish)

DIRECTIONS:

1. Cook the sausage in a medium frying pan over medium heat for a few minutes until properly cooked. Use a wooden spoon to break the meat apart as it cooks. When the sausage is properly cooked and lightly browned, drain off any excess oil before stirring in the marinara sauce.

2. Cover a large, rimmed baking sheet with grease-proof paper, and set the oven to preheat to 375°F, with the wire rack in the center of the oven.

3. Slice the sweet peppers in half lengthwise, and remove the seeds and ribbing to form boats. Arrange the pepper halves on the prepared baking sheet. Divide the cooked sausage mixture between the hollowed-out peppers in even amounts, smoothing out the surface. Season each boat with a sprinkling of Italian seasoning. Top the boats with mozzarella cheese, and garnish with the pepperoni slices; 2 per boat.

4. Place the peppers in the oven for 20-25 minutes, or until the peppers have softened, and the cheese is lightly toasted and bubbling.

5. Serve the peppers hot, sprinkled with the grated parmesan.

Per Serving:
Calories: 287, Fat: 23.7g, Protein: 13.1g, Carbohydrates: 5.2g, Fiber 2.4g, Net Carbohydrates: 2.8g

CRISPY CAULIFLOWER BITES

COOK TIME: 30 MINS | MAKES: 6 SERVINGS

INGREDIENTS:

- 1/2 tsp. Himalayan salt
- 1/2 tsp. ground turmeric
- 1 tsp. garlic powder
- 1/4 cup parmesan cheese, grated
- 8 cups small cauliflower florets, stems trimmed
- 3 tbsp. extra-virgin avocado oil

DIRECTIONS:

1. Set the oven to preheat to 475°F, with the wire rack in the center of the oven.

2. In a large mixing bowl, whisk together the salt, turmeric, garlic powder, and parmesan cheese. Add the cauliflower florets, and drizzle with the oil. Toss the bowl until all of the florets are evenly coated in the spices.

3. Lay the seasoned florets out on a baking sheet, and roast in the oven for 20-25 minutes, or until the cauliflower is fork-tender and lightly toasted.

4. Serve immediately.

Per Serving:
Calories: 110, Fat: 8g, Protein: 4g, Carbohydrates: 8g, Fiber: 3g, Net Carbohydrates: 5g

SIMPLE MOZZARELLA SKEWERS

COOK TIME: 0 MINS | MAKES: 20 SERVINGS

INGREDIENTS:

- 1/4 tsp. Himalayan salt
- 1/4 tsp. freshly ground black pepper
- 1 tsp. dried oregano
- 2 tbsp. white balsamic vinegar
- 2 tbsp. extra-virgin olive oil
- 20 mini fresh mozzarella balls
- 20 cherry tomatoes
- 20 fresh basil leaves

DIRECTIONS:

1. Place the salt, pepper, oregano, vinegar, and oil in a large mixing bowl. Whisk the ingredients until everything is properly combined. Add the mozzarella balls, and toss until they are evenly coated.

2. Divide the seasoned mozzarella balls, cherry tomatoes, and basil leaves onto 20 bamboo skewers. Build the skewers by adding one of each onto the skewer, mozzarella balls, tomatoes, and a basil leaf.

3. Serve immediately.

Per Serving:
Calories: 95, Fat: 8g, Protein: 5g, Carbohydrates: 1g, Fiber: 0g, Net Carbohydrates: 1g

SALADS & SIDES

HEARTS OF PALM & AVO SALAD

COOK TIME: 0 MINS | MAKES: 1 SERVING

INGREDIENTS:

- 2 cups salad greens
- 1 heirloom tomato, sliced
- 1/2 cup canned hearts of palm, sliced
- 1/2 Hass avocado, chopped
- 1/4 tsp. Himalayan salt
- 1/4 tsp. freshly ground black pepper
- 1 tsp. freshly squeezed lemon juice
- 1 tbsp. extra-virgin avocado oil

DIRECTIONS:

1. Arrange the salad greens on a plate, and top with the tomato slices, hearts of palm, and avocado. Season with the salt and pepper before drizzling with lemon juice and oil.

2. Serve immediately.

Per Serving:
Calories: 282, Fat: 25g, Protein: 6g, Carbohydrates: 14g, Fiber: 8g, Net Carbohydrates: 6g

FRENCH-STYLE SALMON SALAD

COOK TIME: 10 MINS | MAKES: 2 SERVINGS

INGREDIENTS:

- Himalayan salt
- 1 1/2 cups Haricot Verts, trimmed
- 2 large free-range eggs
- 1 tbsp. coconut oil
- 2 medium salmon fillets, patted dry
- Freshly ground black pepper
- 1/2 tsp. French mustard
- 1 tsp. crushed garlic
- 1 tbsp. freshly squeezed lemon juice
- 3 tbsp. extra virgin olive oil
- 4 cups mixed salad greens
- 1/2 medium red onion, sliced
- 1/2 medium cucumber, sliced
- 2 heirloom tomatoes, sliced
- 2 tbsp. capers
- 8 Kalamata olives, pitted and halved

DIRECTIONS:

1. Bring a large pot of salted water to a rolling boil. Blanch the Haricot Verts in the boiling water for 2-4 minutes until they brighten in color. Immediately use a slotted spoon to remove the Haricot Verts from the boiling water, and dunk them into a bowl of iced water. Drain the Haricot Verts in a colander over the sink, and set aside to dry.

2. In the same boiling water from the Haricot Verts, boil the eggs. Cook for 8-9 minutes for soft yolks, and 13 minutes for hard yolks. Use a slotted spoon to remove the eggs, and dunk them in another ice bath to stop the cooking process. Peel and chop the eggs once they have cooled, and set aside.

3. Heat the coconut oil in a large frying pan over medium-high heat. Season both sides of each salmon fillet with a pinch of salt and pepper while the pan heats up. When the pan is nice and hot, reduce the heat to medium, and fry the fillets for 3-4 minutes per side, until the salmon is opaque. If the fish is not lifting easily, allow it a few more minutes to cook; do not try and pry the fish off the pan. Transfer the cooked salmon to a plate.

4. In a small glass bowl, whisk together the mustard, garlic, lemon juice, olive oil, and a small pinch of salt and pepper.

5. Divide the salad greens between 2 plates, and top each salad with red onion, cucumber, and tomatoes. Arrange the blanched Haricot Verts on the salads, and top with the cooked salmon. You may first remove the salmon skin if desired.

6. Garnish the fillets with capers, olives, and chopped egg before drizzling with the salad dressing.

7. Serve immediately.

Per Serving:
Calories: 605, Fat: 44.4g, Protein: 39.1g, Carbohydrates: 12.5g, Fiber: 4.3g, Net Carbohydrates: 8.2g

CHEESY BUFFALO CHICKEN SALAD

COOK TIME: 0 MINS | MAKES: 6 SERVINGS

INGREDIENTS:

- 2 cups frozen cauliflower florets
- 3/4 cup crumbled cooked bacon
- 4 cups shredded cooked chicken
- 2 tbsp. ranch seasoning mix
- 1 tbsp. freshly squeezed lemon juice
- 1/4 cup sour cream
- 1/3 cup buffalo wing sauce
- 1 cup mayonnaise
- 3 spring onions, sliced
- 4 oz. grated mozzarella cheese
- 1/4 tsp. Himalayan salt
- 1/4 tsp. freshly ground black pepper

DIRECTIONS:

1. Steam or cook the cauliflower florets according to package instructions. Strain the cooked cauliflower through a colander set over the sink, and allow to drain for a few minutes. Place the drained cauliflower in a clean kitchen towel, and press as much water out as possible.

2. Transfer the cauliflower to a large mixing bowl, along with the cooked bacon and chicken.

3. Place the ranch seasoning, lemon juice, sour cream, buffalo wing sauce, and mayonnaise in a medium-sized mixing bowl. Whisk the ingredients together until everything is properly combined.

4. Scrape the sauce into the bowl of cauliflower, bacon, and chicken, stirring until everything is properly combined.

5. Add the spring onions, cheese, salt, and pepper, stirring to combine.

6. Cover the salad, and chill for 1 hour before serving.

Quick Tip:
Any leftovers can be refrigerated in an airtight container for no more than 3 days.

Per Serving:
Calories: 432, Fat: 32.9g, Protein: 31.8g, Carbohydrates: 6.2g, Fiber: 2.7g, Net Carbohydrates: 3.5g

SPICY CORIANDER CHICKEN SALAD

COOK TIME: 0 MINS | MAKES: 4 SERVINGS

INGREDIENTS:

- 2 cups cooked chicken, shredded
- 1/8 tsp. Himalayan salt
- 1/8 tsp. freshly ground black pepper
- 1/2 tsp. garlic powder
- 1/2 cup mayonnaise
- 1/4 cup celery, chopped
- 3 tbsp. freshly squeezed lime juice
- 2 tbsp. chipotle peppers in adobe sauce, chopped
- 2 tbsp. red onions, finely chopped
- 2 tbsp. fresh coriander leaves, chopped
- 1 tsp. sweet smoked paprika

DIRECTIONS:

1. In a large mixing bowl, stir together the chicken, salt, pepper, garlic powder, mayonnaise, celery, lime juice, chipotle peppers, red onion, and coriander leaves until all of the ingredients are properly combined.

2. Cover the bowl with cling wrap, and chill for 30 minutes before serving.

3. Sprinkle the paprika over the salad. Serve and enjoy!

Per Serving:
Calories: 246, Fat: 38.2g, Protein: 21.3g, Carbohydrates: 3.2g, Fiber: 1.4g, Net Carbohydrates: 1.8g

SHRIMP-STUFFED AVOCADOS

COOK TIME: 0 MINS | MAKES: 2 SERVINGS

INGREDIENTS:

- 1 tsp. Himalayan salt
- 1/8 tsp. freshly ground black pepper
- 1 tsp. garlic powder
- 2 tsp. dried minced onion
- 2 tbsp. freshly squeezed lime juice
- 1/4 cup sour cream
- 1/3 cup mayonnaise
- 1/3 cup heirloom tomatoes, chopped
- 4 oz. canned tiny shrimp, drained
- 1/3 cup English cucumber, peeled and chopped
- 1 large Hass avocado

DIRECTIONS:

1. In a small glass bowl, whisk together the salt, pepper, garlic powder, dried minced onion, lime juice, sour cream, and mayonnaise.

2. In a large mixing bowl, toss together the tomatoes, shrimp, and cumber. Scrape the dressing over the salad, and stir to combine. Cover the bowl in cling wrap, and refrigerate for 20-30 minutes.

3. Once the salad is properly chilled, halve the avocado and discard the pip. Divide the salad between the avocado halves, and serve.

Quick Tip:
Any leftovers can be refrigerated in an airtight container for no more than 3 days.

Per Serving:
Calories: 361, Fat: 28.4g, Protein: 27.5g, Carbohydrates: 5.4g, Fiber: 2.3g, Net Carbohydrates: 3.1g

CRISPY VEG TOSSED SALAD

COOK TIME: 15 MINS | MAKES: 2 SERVINGS

INGREDIENTS:

- 2 tbsp. extra-virgin olive oil
- 1 tsp. crushed garlic
- 2 tbsp. red onions, chopped
- 2 tbsp. celery, chopped
- 1/4 cup purple cabbage, chopped
- 1/3 cup sweet peppers, chopped
- 1/3 cup button mushrooms, sliced
- 1/2 cup cauliflower florets, chopped
- 3/4 cup broccoli florets, chopped
- 4 grape tomatoes, halved
- 1/3 cup kale leaves
- 8 oz. cooked chicken, chopped
- 1/4 tsp. Himalayan salt
- 1/8 tsp. freshly ground black pepper
- 2 tbsp. soy sauce

DIRECTIONS:

1. In a large frying pan over medium-high heat, heat the olive oil. When the oil is nice and hot, fry the garlic, red onions, celery, cabbage, sweet peppers, mushrooms, cauliflower, and broccoli for 8-10 minutes, or until the vegetables soften, and crisp around the edges.

2. When the vegetables are nice and crisp, add the tomatoes, kale, and chicken to the pan, frying for 3-5 additional minutes, until the kale has reduced in size and the chicken is heated through. Season the vegetables with the salt and pepper.

3. Divide the cooked vegetables between 2 plates, and drizzle each plate with 1 tablespoon of soy sauce before serving.

Per Serving:
Calories: 332, Fat: 17.8g, Protein: 24.5g, Carbohydrates: 5.5g, Fiber: 2.4g, Net Carbohydrates: 3.1g

SUMMER FLORETS SALAD

COOK TIME: 0 MINS | MAKES: 6-8 SERVINGS

INGREDIENTS:

- 10 slices bacon, cooked and crumbled
- 1/2 cup roasted and salted shelled sunflower seeds
- 1 cup sharp cheddar cheese, grated
- 1/2 cup red onions, finely diced
- 3 cups cauliflower florets, chopped
- 3 cups broccoli florets, chopped
- 1/2 tsp. garlic powder
- 1 1/2 tsp. balsamic vinegar
- ¼ cup granular erythritol
- 1 cup mayonnaise

DIRECTIONS:

1. In a large mixing bowl, toss together the bacon, sunflower seeds, cheddar, red onions, cauliflower, and broccoli until all of the ingredients are properly combined.

2. In a small glass bowl, whisk together the garlic powder, balsamic vinegar, erythritol, and mayonnaise. Pour the sauce over everything in the mixing bowl, and gently stir to coat.

3. Cover the bowl in cling wrap, and chill for a minimum of 4 hours before serving.

Quick Tip:
Any leftovers can be refrigerated in an airtight container for no more than 4 days.

Per Serving:
Calories: 277, Fat: 21.3g, Protein: 14.6g, Carbohydrates: 8.7g, Fiber: 3.3g, Net Carbohydrates: 5.4g

NUTTY CHICKEN & HERB SALAD

COOK TIME: 0 MINS | MAKES: 2 SERVINGS

INGREDIENTS:

- 1/2 tsp. Himalayan salt
- 1/4 tsp. freshly ground black pepper
- 1 tbsp. yellow curry powder
- 1 tbsp. fresh mint leaves, chopped
- 1 tbsp. fresh coriander leaves, chopped
- 3 tbsp. raw shelled pumpkin seeds
- 1/3 cup mayonnaise
- 1/2 cup small green apples, chopped
- 2 cups cooked chicken, chopped

DIRECTIONS:

1. In a large mixing bowl, combine the salt, pepper, curry powder, mint, coriander, pumpkin seeds, mayonnaise, apples, and chicken.

2. Serve the salad right away, or chill until ready to serve.

Quick Tip:
Any leftovers can be refrigerated in an airtight container for no more than 5 days.

Per Serving:
Calories: 246, Fat: 19g, Protein: 19g, Carbohydrates: 2g, Fiber: 0g, Net Carbohydrates: 2g

ARTICHOKE & KALE BOWLS

COOK TIME: 5 MINS | MAKES: 6 SERVINGS

INGREDIENTS:

- 14 oz. canned artichoke hearts, drained and chopped
- 8 oz. cream cheese
- 10 oz. frozen kale, cooked and drained
- 1/8 tsp. Himalayan salt
- 1/8 tsp. freshly ground black pepper
- 1/2 tsp. garlic powder
- 1 tsp. onion powder
- 1/3 cup mayonnaise
- 1 1/2 cups parmesan cheese, grated

DIRECTIONS:

1. In a large glass bowl, microwave the artichoke hearts, cream cheese, and kale on 70% for 1 minute, or until the cream cheese is soft enough to mix. Use a wooden spoon to stir the ingredients until everything is properly combined. If the cheese is not yet soft enough, return the bowl to the microwave at 30-second intervals, stirring until you have the right consistency.

2. When the cream cheese is soft enough and the ingredients are properly mixed through, add the salt, pepper, garlic powder, onion powder, and mayonnaise, stirring to combine. Finally, add the parmesan cheese, and lightly mix through. Return the bowl to the microwave for 1 additional minute, until the mixture is creamy.

3. Stir well before serving.

Quick Tip:
Any leftovers can be refrigerated in an airtight container for no more than 5 days.

Per Serving:
Calories: 302, Fat: 23.8g, Protein: 18.2g, Carbohydrates: 4.7g, Fiber: 2.9g, Net Carbohydrates: 1.8g

PESTO-COATED CAULIFLOWER FLORETS

COOK TIME: 8 MINS | MAKES: 8 SERVINGS

INGREDIENTS:

- 2 tbsp. extra-virgin olive oil
- 4 cups cauliflower florets, chopped
- 1/4 tsp. cayenne pepper (optional)
- 1/2 cup ready-made pesto sauce
- 1/4 cup parmesan cheese, grated

DIRECTIONS:

1. In a large frying pan over high heat, heat the olive oil. When the oil is nice and hot, toss and fry the florets for a few minutes, until the edges are nice and crispy. Stir in the cayenne pepper and pesto sauce before transferring the pan to a wooden chopping board. Cover the pan with a fitted lid, and let stand for 5-10 minutes until the cauliflower has softened.

2. Garnish the cauliflower with parmesan before serving hot.

Quick Tip:
Any leftovers can be refrigerated in an airtight container for no more than 3 days.

Per Serving:
Calories: 86, Fat: 6.5g, Protein: 3.8g, Carbohydrates: 3.2g, Fiber: 1.3g, Net Carbohydrates: 1.9g

CHEESY JALAPEÑO & SAUSAGE BAKE

COOK TIME: 20 MINS | MAKES: 6 SERVINGS

INGREDIENTS:

- 1/2 tsp. garlic powder
- 1 1/2 cups mozzarella cheese, grated (divided)
- 8 oz. packaged cream cheese, softened
- 1 spring onion, chopped
- 1 cup red bell peppers, chopped
- 2 jalapeño peppers, seeded and chopped
- 4 oz. button mushrooms, chopped
- 1 lb. Italian sausage, browned and drained of oil

DIRECTIONS:

1. Set the oven to preheat to 350°F, with the wire rack in the center of the oven.

2. Place the garlic powder, 1 cup of mozzarella, and cream cheese in a large mixing bowl, and use a wooden spoon to thoroughly combine the ingredients. Stir in the spring onion, bell peppers, jalapeños, mushrooms, and sausage. Scrape the thick mixture into a large casserole dish, smoothing out the top. Sprinkle the remaining mozzarella over the top in an even layer.

3. Place the dish in the oven for 20-25 minutes, or until the cheese is lightly toasted and bubbling. Allow the dish to cool for 5-10 minutes before serving.

Quick Tip:
Any leftovers can be refrigerated in an airtight container for no more than 4 days. Use an oven or microwave on the lowest setting to reheat the dish.

Per Serving:
Calories: 260, Fat: 22.8g, Protein: 10.9g, Carbohydrates: 3.9g, Fiber: 0.8g, Net Carbohydrates: 3.1g

CREAMY SUMMER CUCUMBER SALAD

COOK TIME: 0 MINS | MAKES: 4 SERVINGS

INGREDIENTS:

- 1/4 tsp. Himalayan salt
- 1/4 tsp. freshly ground black pepper
- 1 tsp. dried dill weed
- 1 tsp. white vinegar
- 1/4 cup mayonnaise
- 1/2 cup sour cream
- 1/4 cup red onions, sliced
- 1 large English cucumber, peeled and sliced
- Fresh parsley, chopped (for garnish)

DIRECTIONS:

1. In a small glass bowl, whisk together the salt, pepper, dill weed, vinegar, mayonnaise, and sour cream. Set aside.

2. Place the red onions in a large mixing bowl. Use paper towels to pat any excess water off the cucumber slices before adding them to the bowl. Toss to combine.

3. Scrape the sour cream and mayonnaise mixture into the large bowl, and stir until all of the ingredients are evenly coated. Cover the bowl in cling wrap, and refrigerate for a minimum of 30 minutes before serving.

4. Serve garnished with fresh parsley.

Quick Tip:
Any leftovers can be refrigerated in an airtight container for no more than 4 days.

Per Serving:
Calories: 125, Fat: 11g, Protein: 1.4g, Carbohydrates: 3.9g, Fiber: 0.8g, Net Carbohydrates: 3.1g

SIMPLE SPICY CHICKEN SALAD

COOK TIME: 0 MINS | MAKES: 2 SERVINGS

INGREDIENTS:

- 1/3 cup mayonnaise
- 1/2 cup celery, thinly sliced
- 2 cups cooked chicken, chopped
- 2 tbsp. Louisiana-style hot sauce
- 1/4 tsp. Himalayan salt
- 1/4 tsp. freshly ground black pepper

DIRECTIONS:

1. In a large mixing bowl, stir together the mayonnaise, celery, chicken, hot sauce, salt, and pepper. Chill the salad before serving, or serve as is at room temperature.

Quick Tip:
Any leftovers can be refrigerated in an airtight container for no more than 5 days.

Per Serving:
Calories: 173, Fat: 14g, Protein: 13g, Carbohydrates: 3.3g, Fiber: 1.2g, Net Carbohydrates: 2.1g

LETTUCE-WRAPPED CHICKEN SANDWICH

COOK TIME: 0 MINS | MAKES: 1 SERVING

INGREDIENTS:

- 2 large iceberg lettuce leaves
- 2 tbsp. mayonnaise
- 2 slices cooked bacon
- 4 thick wedges heirloom tomato
- 2 oz. cooked chicken, shredded
- 1/4 tsp. Himalayan salt
- 1/8 tsp. freshly ground black pepper

DIRECTIONS:

1. Place a large piece of greaseproof paper on a clean counter or chopping board. Arrange the lettuce leaves in the center of the sheet, with 1 leaf about 1/3 over the other.

2. Spoon the mayonnaise onto 1 edge of the leaves in a straight line of about 8-inches long. Place the bacon strips on the mayonnaise, followed by the tomatoes and chicken. Season the chicken with salt and pepper before carefully rolling the leaves up like a burrito, starting with the edge that has the line of ingredients.

3. Roll the sandwich tightly in the greaseproof paper, and fold the edges over. Cut the roll in half, and serve immediately, removing the paper as you eat.

Per Serving:
Calories: 354, Fat: 29g, Protein: 19g, Carbohydrates: 5g, Fiber: 2g, Net Carbohydrates: 3g

ITALIAN-STYLE EGGPLANT BAKE

COOK TIME: 20 MINS | MAKES: 6 SERVINGS

INGREDIENTS:

- 20 oz. frozen kale, thawed and chopped
- 2 large free-range eggs
- Himalayan salt
- 2 tbsp. Italian seasoning blend
- 1 1/2 cups whole-milk ricotta cheese
- 3/4 cup no-sugar-added marinara sauce
- 1 large eggplant, thinly sliced into rounds
- 3 tbsp. extra-virgin olive oil
- 2 cups shredded, whole milk mozzarella cheese
- 1/2 cup parmesan cheese, grated
- Fresh basil leaves, chopped (for garnish)

DIRECTIONS:

1. Set the oven to preheat to 450°F, with the wire rack in the center of the oven.

2. Place the thawed kale in a colander set over the sink, and use the back of a wooden spoon to press as much water out of the kale as possible.

3. In a large mixing bowl, lightly beat the eggs. Add the kale, and stir to combine. Add 1 teaspoon of salt, the Italian seasoning, and the ricotta cheese, stirring to combine.

4. Spoon 2 tablespoons of the marinara sauce into a large baking dish, in an even layer that coats the bottom. Arrange 1/3 of the eggplant slices over the sauce; some of the slices may need to overlap to fit. Use a basting brush to coat the slices with 1 tablespoon of olive oil. Sprinkle a pinch of salt over the oiled eggplant slices. Scoop 1/3 of the ricotta cheese and kale mixture over the eggplant, and use an offset spatula to smooth it out. Sprinkle 1/2 cup of mozzarella over the ricotta cheese, followed by half of the remaining marinara sauce in an even layer.

5. Starting with the eggplants, repeat the layers with the remaining ingredients, until you have 3 sets of layers.

6. Sprinkle the parmesan over the top of the dish in an even layer.

7. Bake in the oven for 18-20 minutes, or until the cheese is lightly toasted and bubbling.

8. Allow the dish to cool for 5 minutes, before garnishing with the basil leaves and serving.

Per Serving:
Calories: 432, Fat: 31g, Protein: 25g, Carbohydrates: 17g, Fiber 5.6g, Net Carbohydrates: 11,4g

MEATY STUFFED BELL PEPPERS

COOK TIME: 20 MINS | MAKES: 4 SERVINGS

INGREDIENTS:

- 2 tsp. extra-virgin olive oil
- 1/2 small onion, diced
- 2 cloves crushed garlic
- 1/2 lb. fresh Italian sausage links, casings removed
- 1/2 lb. ground beef
- 1/2 tsp. Himalayan salt
- 1/4 tsp. freshly ground black pepper
- 1/2 tsp. dried oregano
- 1 tbsp. tomato paste
- 2 large bell peppers of any color
- 8 oz. mozzarella cheese, grated
- 1/4 cup parmesan cheese, grated
- 8 thin slices pepperoni

DIRECTIONS:

1. Set the oven to preheat to 425°F, with the wire rack in the center of the oven.

2. Heat the olive oil in a large frying pan over medium heat. When the oil is nice and hot, fry the onions for about 3 minutes until softened. Add the garlic to the pan, and fry for 1 additional minute, until fragrant.

3. Add the sausage, beef, salt, pepper, and oregano to the pan, and fry for about 6 minutes, using a wooden spoon to break the meat and sausage apart as it cooks. When the meat is just about cooked, stir in the tomato paste. Allow the meat to cook completely while stirring. Once the meat is properly cooked, taste the sauce, and add additional salt and pepper if desired.

4. Slice the bell peppers in half lengthwise with a sharp knife, to form 4 boats. Scoop the insides out with a spoon, before placing the boats, open side up, in a medium or large casserole dish. The size of the dish will depend on the size of the peppers, as you want them to fit snuggly, and not roll around. If you would like the pepper boats to be completely soft, place them in the oven for 5 minutes before continuing. Leave out this step if you would prefer them to be slightly crunchier.

5. Divide the cooked meat into 8 even portions, and do the same with the mozzarella. Fill each bell pepper with 1 portion of the cooked meat, and top with 1 portion of mozzarella. Repeat the process with the remaining portions of meat and mozzarella. Top each filled pepper with parmesan and 2 slices of pepperoni.

6. Place the casserole dish in the oven for 20 minutes, or until the cheese is bubbling and the peppers are fork-tender, but still crisp. You may also place the dish under the broiler for 1-2 minutes to get a nice toast.

7. Serve the stuffed peppers hot, and enjoy.

Per Serving:
Calories: 566, Fat: 39g, Protein: 39g, Carbohydrates: 12g, Fiber: 1.8g, Net Carbohydrates: 10,2g

FISH & SEAFOOD

ONE-PAN SEA BASS BAKE

COOK TIME: 20 MINS | MAKES: 4 SERVINGS

INGREDIENTS:

- 2 cloves crushed garlic
- 1/4 cup duck fat, melted
- 1/4 cup mixed fresh herbs, chopped (basil, rosemary, thyme, and oregano)
- 1 small red onion, diced
- 5 oz. tomatoes, diced
- 5 oz. broccoli florets
- 1 medium red bell pepper, diced
- 2 medium zucchini, sliced
- 1 small eggplant, thinly sliced
- Himalayan salt
- Freshly ground black pepper
- 4 medium sea bass fillets
- 1 lemon, sliced
- 2 tbsp. extra-virgin avocado oil
- 1/2 tsp. French mustard
- 1 tsp. garlic powder
- 1 tbsp. freshly squeezed lemon juice
- 3 tbsp. extra-virgin olive oil
- 1/4 cup fresh parsley, chopped (for garnish)

DIRECTIONS:

1. Set the oven to preheat to 400°F, with the wire rack in the center of the oven.

2. In a large mixing bowl, whisk together the garlic and melted duck fat, then add in the fresh herbs. Add the onions, tomatoes, broccoli, bell pepper, zucchini, eggplant, and a pinch of salt and pepper. Toss until all the ingredients are evenly coated. Lay the seasoned vegetables out on a large, rimmed baking tray, and bake in the oven for 15 minutes.

3. Remove the tray from the oven, flip the vegetables, and increase the heat to 475°F. Season both sides of the sea bass fillets with salt and pepper, before nestling them on top of the vegetables with the skins facing up. Arrange the lemon slices on top of the fish. Place the tray back in the oven for 8-12 minutes, or until the fish is properly cooked, and flakes easily when pierced with a fork. If you prefer crispy skin, place the fish under the broiler for the last few minutes of cooking.

4. While the fish cooks, whisk together the mustard, garlic powder, lemon juice, and olive oil in a small glass bowl.

5. Drizzle the avocado oil over the cooked fish, and serve, garnished with the fresh parsley leaves, and with the dressing on the side.

Quick Tip:
Any leftovers can be refrigerated in an airtight container for no more than 3 days.

Per Serving:
Calories: 447, Fat: 32.5g, Protein: 26.4g, Carbohydrates: 8.7g, Fiber: 4.9g, Net Carbohydrates: 8.7g

GRILLED, CURRIED SHRIMP

COOK TIME: 50 MINS | MAKES: 4 SERVINGS

INGREDIENTS:

- Himalayan salt
- Freshly ground black pepper
- 1 tsp. lemon zest, finely grated
- 1/4 tsp. crushed red pepper flakes
- 1 tsp. ground turmeric
- 2 tsp. garam masala
- 2 tsp. fresh ginger, grated and peeled
- 1 clove garlic, crushed
- 1/2 cup plain Greek yogurt
- 1 lb. large shrimp, peeled and deveined
- 3 tbsp. freshly squeezed lemon juice
- Fresh coriander leaves, chopped (for serving)
- Red onion, thinly sliced (for serving)
- 1 lemon, quartered

DIRECTIONS:

1. In a large mixing bowl, whisk together 1/4 teaspoon each of salt and pepper, along with the lemon zest, red pepper flakes, turmeric, masala, ginger, garlic, and yogurt. Stir in the shrimp until it is evenly coated. Cover the bowl in cling wrap, and chill for 30 minutes.

2. When the shrimp is properly chilled, preheat the grill on medium heat. Add the lemon juice to the bowl, and stir to combine. Arrange the shrimp on bamboo skewers, before grilling for 2-3 minutes per side, or until the shrimp are no longer translucent.

3. Arrange the cooked skewers on a plate, and garnish with the fresh coriander leaves and red onions. Serve the shrimp with the lemon wedges on the side.

Per Serving:
Calories: 135, Fat: 2.5g, Protein: 21g, Carbohydrates: 6g, Fiber: 1g, Net Carbohydrates: 5g

PAN-SEARED SALMON PATTIES

COOK TIME: 8 MINS | MAKES: 6 SERVINGS

INGREDIENTS:

- 1 tsp. soy sauce
- 2 tsp. freshly squeezed lemon juice
- 2 tsp. dried parsley
- 2 tsp. dried minced onion
- 2 large free-range eggs, beaten
- 1/4 cup parmesan cheese, grated
- 1/3 cup pork panko
- 1/3 cup mayonnaise
- 15 oz. canned salmon, drained
- 2 tbsp. extra-virgin olive oil
- Fresh parsley, chopped (for garnish)
- 1 lemon, cut into wedges

DIRECTIONS:

1. In a large mixing bowl, stir together the soy sauce, lemon juice, dried parsley, minced onion, eggs, parmesan, pork panko, mayonnaise, and salmon. When all of the ingredients are properly combined, use clean hands to shape the mixture into 12 patties of roughly the same size. They should be about 1/4-inch thick.

2. In a large frying pan over medium heat, heat the olive oil. When the oil is nice and hot, reduce the heat to medium-low, and fry the patties in batches. Cook for 4-6 minutes per side, or until the patties are cooked all the way through, and have a nice sear on each side.

3. Serve the patties hot, garnished with fresh parsley, and with lemon wedges on the side.

Quick Tip:
Any leftovers can be refrigerated in an airtight container for no more than 4 days.

Per Serving:
Calories: 418, Fat: 38.5g, Protein: 20.4g, Carbohydrates: 10g, Fiber: 2.5g, Net Carbohydrates: 7.5g

OVEN-ROASTED SALMON & BOK CHOY

COOK TIME: 15 MINS | MAKES: 4 SERVINGS

INGREDIENTS:

- 4 jalapeño chilies, seeded and thinly sliced
- 1 bunch spring onions, thinly sliced
- 5 celery stalks, thinly sliced
- 1 tbsp. extra virgin olive oil
- 1/8 tsp. Himalayan salt
- 4 skinless salmon fillets
- 2 tbsp. low-sodium soy sauce
- Steamed Bok choy for serving
- 1/4 cup unsalted peanuts, chopped

DIRECTIONS:

1. Set the oven to preheat to 450°F, with the wire rack in the center of the oven.

2. Place the chilies, spring onions, and celery on a large, rimmed baking sheet. Drizzle everything with the oil and salt. Toss the vegetables until they are evenly coated in oil and salt. Roast in the oven for 15 minutes, stirring half way through the cooking time.

3. Arrange the salmon fillets, skin-side down, in a large baking dish, and drizzle with the soy sauce. Bake in the oven for 12 minutes, or until the fish is cooked all the way through, and no longer translucent.

4. Serve the salmon fillets on a bed of steamed Bok choy and roasted vegetables, garnished with peanuts.

Per Serving:
Calories: 335, Fat: 14g, Protein: 39g, Carbohydrates: 11g, Fiber: 4g, Net Carbohydrates: 7g

CRUNCHY, ALMOND-COATED SALMON

COOK TIME: 15 MINS | MAKES: 4 SERVINGS

INGREDIENTS:

- 1 lb. Haricot Verts, trimmed
- 1/2 tsp. Himalayan salt
- 1/2 tsp. freshly ground black pepper
- 1 tbsp. extra-virgin olive oil
- 1 tsp. lemon zest, finely grated
- 2 tsp. Creole seasoning
- 1 cup plain Greek yogurt
- 4 skinless salmon fillets
- 1 cup sliced almonds, coarsely chopped
- Olive oil cooking spray

DIRECTIONS:

1. Line a large, rimmed baking tray with aluminum foil, and set the oven to preheat to 450°F, with the wire rack in the center of the oven.

2. Toss the Haricot Verts on the prepared baking tray, along with the salt, pepper, and oil, until evenly coated. Spread the Haricot Verts out in an even layer, and bake in the oven for 10 minutes.

3. In a medium-sized mixing bowl, whisk together the lemon zest, Creole seasoning, and yogurt. Dip the salmon fillets in the yogurt mixture, and then into the crushed almonds. Place the coated fillets on the baking tray beside the Haricot Verts. Coat the fillets in olive oil cooking spray before returning the tray to the oven for 12 minutes, or until the fish is properly cooked, and the Haricot Verts are fork-tender.

Per Serving:
Calories: 310, Fat: 13g, Protein: 39g, Carbohydrates: 9g, Fiber: 4g, Net Carbohydrates: 5g

SPICY ROASTED SHRIMP SALAD

COOK TIME: 20 MINS | MAKES: 4 SERVINGS

INGREDIENTS:

- 3 poblano peppers, seeded and diced
- 2 medium onions, sliced
- 2 tsp. chili powder
- 1 tbsp. extra-virgin olive oil
- 1 lb. peeled and deveined large shrimp
- 2 1/2 oz. mixed salad greens
- 1/2 tsp. Himalayan salt
- 3 tbsp. freshly squeezed lime juice
- 4 radishes, sliced
- 1 large Hass avocado, thinly sliced

DIRECTIONS:

1. Set the oven to preheat to 450°F, with the wire rack in the center of the oven.

2. In a large bowl, toss together the peppers, onions, chili powder, and olive oil, until the vegetables are evenly coated. Spread the peppers and onions out on a large baking sheet, and bake in the oven for 15 minutes.

3. Remove the sheet from the oven, and push the peppers and onions to the side. Place the shrimp on the sheet, and bake in the oven for 5 additional minutes. The shrimp should blush and curl slightly.

4. Allow the baking sheet to cool slightly before scraping everything into a large mixing bowl. Add the salad greens, salt, lime juice, and radishes to the bowl, tossing to combine.

5. Garnish the salad with the avocado slices, and serve.

Per Serving:
Calories: 215, Fat: 12g, Protein: 17g, Carbohydrates: 9g, Fiber: 2g, Net Carbohydrates: 7g

CRAB & SNAPPER ROLLED SKEWERS

COOK TIME: 18 MINS | MAKES: 4 SERVINGS

INGREDIENTS:

- 3 tbsp. extra-virgin olive oil (divided)
- 1 whole garlic clove, chopped
- 1 small onion, chopped
- 2 cups Haricot Verts, roughly chopped
- Himalayan salt
- 1/2 lemon, juiced
- 4 oz. crab meat
- 4 thin snapper fillets, skins removed
- Freshly ground black pepper
- 1/2 cup crumbled feta cheese
- 1 tbsp. melted butter
- 1/2 cup cherry tomatoes

DIRECTIONS:

1. Coat a large, rimmed baking tray with 1 tablespoon of olive oil, and set the oven to preheat to 450°F, with the wire rack in the center of the oven.

2. Heat 1 tablespoon of olive oil in a large frying pan over medium heat. When the oil is nice and hot, fry the garlic and onions for about 2 minutes, or until they just start to caramelize. Stir in the chopped Haricots Verts, and fry while stirring for an additional 2 minutes. Transfer the pan to a wooden chopping board, and add 1/4 teaspoon of salt, the lemon juice, and the crabmeat, stirring to combine. Taste the mixture, and add more salt if desired.

3. Place the fillets on a clean chopping board, and season both sides with salt and pepper to taste. Divide the crab mixture between the 4 fillets, spreading it over the top of each fillet, and leaving about an inch of space at 1 end. Sprinkle the crumbled feta over the filling on each fillet, leaving 4 tablespoons to sprinkle over the rolled skewers. Starting at 1 end and working your way towards the end with the open inch, roll the fillets up, like a cinnamon roll, as tightly as you can without spilling any filling. Use a skewer to pin the edge to the roll. Arrange the rolled skewers on your prepared baking tray. Carefully pour the melted butter over the rolled skewers, and sprinkle each with 1 tablespoon of feta cheese.

4. In a small mixing bowl, toss the cherry tomatoes with the final tablespoon of olive oil. Scatter the coated tomatoes on the tray, around the rolled snapper skewers.

5. Place the tray in the oven for 15 minutes, or until the fish is opaque. Serve the rolled skewers with the roasted tomatoes on the side.

Per Serving:
Calories: 363, Fat: 19g, Protein: 45g, Carbohydrates: 6g, Fiber 1g, Net Carbohydrates: 5g

SHRIMP & ZUCCHINI NOODLES

COOK TIME: 8 MINS | MAKES: 4 SERVINGS

INGREDIENTS:

- 1/4 cup butter
- 1/2 tsp. Himalayan salt
- 1/4 tsp. freshly ground black pepper
- 1 tbsp. lemon zest, finely grated
- 2 tbsp. capers, drained
- 1 lb. large shrimp, peeled and deveined
- 4 cups zucchini noodles
- 2 tbsp. fresh parsley, chopped
- 1 lemon, quartered (for serving)

DIRECTIONS:

1. In a large frying pan over medium-high heat, melt the butter. When the butter is bubbling, add the salt, pepper, lemon zest, and capers, frying for about 1 minute, until the flavors have released.

2. Add the shrimp to the pan, and stir for about 3 minutes, until the shrimp just begin to blush.

3. Stir in the zucchini noodles for an additional 3 minutes, until the strands become tender and the shrimp tails curl into a C.

4. Plate the shrimp and zucchini noodles, and garnish with the parsley and lemon quarters before serving.

Per Serving:
Calories: 237, Fat: 14g, Protein: 24g, Carbohydrates: 4g, Fiber: 1g, Net Carbohydrates: 3g

FRIED HADDOCK IN CURRY SAUCE

COOK TIME: 15 MINS | MAKES: 4 SERVINGS

INGREDIENTS:

Haddock:

- 1 lb. haddock fillets, skins removed
- 1/2 tsp. Himalayan salt
- 1/4 tsp. freshly ground black pepper
- 1/2 tsp. sweet smoked paprika
- 1/2 tsp. garlic powder
- 1/3 cup sun-flour
- 1 large free-range egg, beaten
- 1/4 cup extra-virgin olive oil
- 1/4 cup fresh coriander leaves, chopped (for garnish)

Curry Sauce:

- 1 tbsp. avocado oil
- 2 tbsp. red curry paste
- 1 tsp. red pepper flakes
- 1 tbsp. no-sugar-added fish sauce
- 1 cup canned coconut milk

DIRECTIONS:

1. On a clean chopping board, slice the haddock into 4 equal portions.

2. In a large mixing bowl, whisk together the salt, pepper, paprika, garlic powder, and flour. Place the egg in a separate shallow dish.

3. Heat the oil in a large frying pan over medium heat. Dredge the fish pieces in the spiced flour, tapping off any excess. Dip the coated fish in the egg, and then back in the flour to make a nice, thick coating. Carefully lower the fish into the hot oil, and fry for 3 minutes per side, or until the coating is a golden brown. Set the cooked fish aside on a paper-towel-lined plate while you prepare the rest of the dish. Wipe the pan clean using paper towels or greaseproof paper.

4. Use the clean frying pan to heat the avocado oil over medium heat. When the oil is nice and hot, stir in the curry paste for 1 minute, until the fragrance is released. Stir in the red pepper flakes, fish sauce, and coconut milk. Allow the sauce to simmer and thicken for 5 minutes, stirring at regular intervals to prevent burning.

5. Lower the heat, and simmer the cooked fish in the sauce for 2-3 minutes, or until heated through.

6. Serve the fish with the sauce spooned over, and garnished with the fresh coriander leaves.

Per Serving:

Calories: 356, Fat: 26g, Protein: 25g, Carbohydrates: 6g, Fiber: 1g, Net Carbohydrates: 5g

CREAMY COCONUT SHRIMP STEW

COOK TIME: 10 MINS | MAKES: 4 SERVINGS

INGREDIENTS:

- 1/4 cup extra-virgin avocado oil
- 1/4 cup diced onions
- 1 garlic clove, crushed
- 1/4 cup roasted red peppers, diced
- 1/4 cup fresh coriander leaves, chopped
- 14 oz. canned diced tomatoes with chilies
- 1 1/2 lbs. extra-large shrimp, peeled and deveined
- 2 tbsp. sriracha sauce
- 1 cup canned coconut milk
- 1 tsp. Himalayan salt
- 1/4 tsp. freshly ground black pepper
- 2 tbsp. freshly squeezed lime juice

DIRECTIONS:

1. In a medium-sized pot over medium heat, heat the avocado oil. When the oil is nice and hot, fry the onions for a few minutes, until they begin to soften and lose their color. Stir in the garlic and roasted red peppers for a few more minutes, until the peppers are tender and the garlic is fragrant.

2. Add the fresh coriander leaves and tomatoes, stirring to combine. Stir in the shrimp for a few minutes, until they blush and are no longer translucent.

3. Stir in the sriracha sauce and coconut milk until heated through, keeping the stew just under a simmer. Transfer the pot to a wooden chopping board, and season with the salt, pepper, and lime juice. Serve hot.

Quick Tip:
Any leftovers can be refrigerated in an airtight container for no more than 5 days. This stew cannot be frozen. To reheat, remove the shrimp from the stew, and heat the sauce before adding the shrimp back, and stirring until just heated. Shrimp becomes rubbery when overcooked.

Per Serving:
Calories: 368, Fat: 24g, Protein: 30g, Carbohydrates: 7g, Fiber: 1g, Net Carbohydrates: 6g

SAUCY STEAK & SHRIMP BOWLS

COOK TIME: 30 MINS | MAKES: 12 SERVINGS

INGREDIENTS:

- 1/2 tsp. garlic powder
- 1 tsp. Himalayan salt
- 1/2 tsp. freshly ground black pepper
- 1 tsp. sweet smoked paprika
- 1 tbsp. ground cumin
- 1 lb. large shrimp, peeled and deveined
- 1 lb. boneless beef steak, thinly sliced
- 2 tbsp. extra-virgin avocado oil
- 8 oz. Spanish-style, dry-cured chorizo, sliced into 1/4-inch rounds
- 1/4 cup finely diced jalapeño peppers
- 1/3 cup red onions, chopped
- 1 tsp. crushed garlic
- 4 cups chicken stock
- 1 cup easy salsa verde
- 2 cups zucchini, roughly chopped
- Fresh coriander leaves, chopped (for garnish)

DIRECTIONS:

1. In a small glass bowl, mix together the garlic powder, salt, pepper, paprika, and cumin.

2. Place the shrimp and beef in 2 separate bowls. Divide the spice mixture between the 2 bowls, and toss to coat the shrimp and beef in the spices.

3. In a large frying pan over medium-high heat, heat the avocado oil. When the oil is nice and hot, fry the chorizo for 5 minutes while stirring, or until the chorizo is properly cooked, and the edges are nicely crisped. Transfer the cooked sausages to a paper-towel-lined plate.

4. Fry the steak in the same pan over high heat for 5 minutes, until the steak is properly cooked and nicely seared on all sides. Scrape the steak onto the plate of chorizo. Add the shrimp to the hot pan, and fry for 3 minutes over medium heat, until the shrimp become opaque. Scrape the cooked shrimp onto the plate of meat.

5. In the same pan, fry the peppers and onions for 5 minutes, until nicely caramelized. Stir in the garlic for 1 minute, until fragrant. Stir in the chicken stock, salsa verde, and zucchini. Once the broth begins to boil, lower the heat and simmer for 10 minutes, stirring at regular intervals to prevent burning. The zucchini should be soft when pierced with a fork.

6. To serve, add about 1/2 cup of shrimp and meat to a bowl, with 1 1/2 cups of broth **per serving**. Garnish the bowls with fresh coriander leaves, and serve hot.

Quick Tip:
Any leftovers can be refrigerated in an airtight container for no more than 5 days.

Per Serving:
Calories: 387, Fat: 22g, Protein: 39g, Carbohydrates: 6g, Fiber: 1g, Net Carbohydrates: 5g

LEMON-DRESSED SEAFOOD PLATTER

COOK TIME: 9 MINS | MAKES: 6 SERVINGS

INGREDIENTS:

- 1 lb. jumbo shrimp, peeled and deveined
- 2 lbs. frozen crab legs, thawed
- 2 lbs. small clams
- 1 lb. frozen calamari rings, thawed
- 1 tsp. Himalayan salt
- 1/4 tsp. freshly ground black pepper
- 1 tsp. crushed garlic
- 2 tbsp. fresh parsley, chopped
- 1 tsp. balsamic vinegar
- 3 tsp. extra-virgin olive oil
- 1/4 cup freshly squeezed lemon juice
- 1 tbsp. lemon zest, finely grated

DIRECTIONS:

1. Bring a full, large pot of salted water to a rolling boil over high heat. When the water is boiling, add the shrimp, crab legs, and clams. Allow the seafood to boil for 7 minutes, or until the majority of the clams have opened. Use a slotted spoon to remove the seafood from the boiling water, and immediately dunk it in iced water. Discard any clams that have not opened after several minutes, as unopened means not good. With the boiling water still on the heat, lower the calamari into the pot, and cook for 2 minutes before transferring to the bowl of ice water, as well.

2. Allow the seafood to cool properly before draining it in a colander set over the sink.

3. In a small glass bowl, whisk together the salt, pepper, garlic, parsley, vinegar, olive oil, lemon juice, and lemon zest.

4. Place the drained seafood in a large mixing bowl, and drizzle the dressing over everything. Toss until all of the seafood is evenly coated in the dressing. Cover the bowl with cling wrap, and chill for a minimum of 1 hour or overnight. Stir the chilled seafood before serving.

Quick Tip:
Any leftovers can be refrigerated in an airtight container for no more than 3 days.

Per Serving:
Calories: 293, Fat: 6g, Protein: 43g, Carbohydrates: 4g, Fiber: 0g, Net Carbohydrates: 4g

COCONUT CURRY BROTH WITH MUSSELS

COOK TIME: 8 MINS | MAKES: 2 SERVINGS

INGREDIENTS:

- 1 tbsp. extra-virgin olive oil
- 1 tsp. red pepper flakes
- 1 tsp. crushed garlic
- 1 tbsp. fresh ginger, grated
- 1 tbsp. red curry paste
- 1 tbsp. coconut aminos
- 2/3 cup canned coconut milk
- 1 lb. mussels, scrubbed and debearded
- 2 tbsp. fresh coriander leaves, chopped (for garnish)
- 1/4 cup spring onions, diced

DIRECTIONS:

1. In a large frying pan over medium-high heat, heat the olive oil. When the oil is nice and hot, fry the red pepper flakes, garlic, and ginger, for 2 minutes, allowing the flavors to meld. Add the curry paste, and stir for 1 additional minute.

2. Stir in the coconut aminos and milk. When everything is properly combined, add the mussels, and cook covered for 7 minutes, or until the majority have opened. Discard any mussels that have not opened after 7 minutes, as unopened means inedible.

3. Spoon the broth and mussels into serving bowls, and garnish with fresh coriander leaves and spring onions before serving hot.

Quick Tip:
Any leftovers can be refrigerated in an airtight container for no more than 2 days. Reheat on the stovetop for 3-5 minutes over medium heat.

Per Serving:
Calories: 443, Fat: 30g, Protein: 32g, Carbohydrates: 6g, Fiber: 1g, Net Carbohydrates: 5g

QUICK & EASY OVEN PAELLA

COOK TIME: 25 MINS | MAKES: 4 SERVINGS

INGREDIENTS:

- 2 tbsp. extra-virgin avocado oil
- 1 lb. boneless chicken breasts, skins removed, cubed
- Himalayan salt
- Freshly ground black pepper
- 8 oz. Spanish-style, dry-cured chorizo
- 1 tsp. crushed garlic
- 1/3 cup chopped sweet peppers
- 1/2 cup onions, chopped
- 2 cups riced cauliflower
- Pinch of saffron threads
- 1/2 tsp. sweet smoked paprika
- 1/4 cup chicken stock
- 1/3 cup frozen peas
- 1/2 cup canned petite diced tomatoes, drained
- 15 mussels, scrubbed and debearded
- 1 lb. jumbo shrimp, peeled and deveined
- 2 tbsp. freshly squeezed lemon juice
- 1 tsp. lemon zest, finely grated
- 1/4 cup fresh parsley, chopped

DIRECTIONS:

1. Use a basting brush to coat a large, rimmed baking tray with the avocado oil, and set the oven to preheat to 400°F, with the wire rack in the center of the oven.

2. Season the chicken cubes with salt and pepper, before arranging them on 1/4 of the prepared baking tray. Arrange the chorizo next to the chicken to make up half of the tray.

3. In a large bowl, toss together the garlic, sweet peppers, onions, and riced cauliflower until everything is properly combined. Spread the vegetables out over the remaining portion of the baking tray, and bake in the oven for 15 minutes.

4. Remove the tray from the oven, scrape the contents into a large mixing bowl, and toss. Add the saffron, paprika, chicken stock, frozen peas, 1 teaspoon of salt, 1/4 teaspoon of pepper, and canned tomatoes, stirring to combine. Carefully pour the contents of the bowl back onto the tray in an even layer. Arrange the mussels and shrimp over everything in the pan in an even layer.

5. Bake in the oven for 10 minutes, until the shrimp blush and their tails curl into a C. Remove the pan from the oven, and discard any mussels that have not opened. Unopened means inedible.

6. Sprinkle the lemon juice over everything in the pan, before garnishing with the lemon zest and parsley. Serve hot.

Quick Tip:
Any leftovers can be refrigerated for no more than 3 days in an airtight container.

Per Serving:
Calories: 476, Fat: 23g, Protein: 56g, Carbohydrates: 10g, Fiber: 3g, Net Carbohydrates: 7g

POULTRY

ITALIAN-STYLE CHICKEN & ZUCCHINI NOODLES

COOK TIME: 10 MINS | MAKES: 4 SERVINGS

INGREDIENTS:

- 3 tbsp. extra-virgin avocado oil
- 2 tsp. crushed garlic
- 2 tbsp. sun-dried tomatoes, chopped
- 1 lb. boneless chicken breasts, skins removed, cubed
- 1 tsp. Himalayan salt
- 1/4 tsp. freshly ground black pepper
- 1/4 tsp. dried oregano leaves
- 1/2 tsp. cayenne pepper
- 6 cups zucchini noodles
- 1/4 cup fresh basil leaves, chopped (for garnish)

DIRECTIONS:

1. In a large frying pan over medium heat, heat the avocado oil. When the oil is nice and hot, stir in the garlic, sun-dried tomatoes, chicken cubes, salt, pepper, oregano, and cayenne pepper.

2. Stir the pan for 5 minutes, until the chicken cubes are properly cooked and nicely browned on all sides.

3. Stir in the zucchini noodles for an additional 5 minutes, or until the noodles are tender when poked with a fork, but still crisp. Plate the chicken and noodles, and serve hot, garnished with fresh basil leaves.

Quick Tip:
Any leftovers can be refrigerated in an airtight container for no more than 5 days.

Per Serving:
Calories: 260, Fat: 12g, Protein: 29g, Carbohydrates: 8g, Fiber: 3g, Net Carbohydrates: 5g

MEDITERRANEAN CHICKEN KEBABS

COOK TIME: 10 MINS | MAKES: 4 SERVINGS

INGREDIENTS:

- Himalayan salt
- Freshly ground black pepper
- 1/2 tsp. dried oregano
- 1/2 tsp. ground cilantro seeds
- 3 tbsp. avocado oil (divided)
- 1 lb. boneless chicken breasts, skins removed, cubed
- 2 whole cloves of garlic, chopped
- 1-pint cherry tomatoes
- 3 tbsp. freshly squeezed lemon juice
- 1/2 cup dill, chopped
- 4 spring onions, thinly sliced
- 1/2 head romaine lettuce
- 1 lemon, sliced into wedges, for serving

DIRECTIONS:

1. Set a grill to preheat on medium-high. In a large mixing bowl, whisk together 1/4 teaspoon of salt, 1/4 teaspoon of pepper, the oregano, cilantro seeds, and 1 tablespoon of oil. Add the chicken cubes, and stir until the cubes are evenly coated in spice. Divide the chicken cubes between a 4 bamboo skewers, and thread them on, leaving enough room on each end for handles.

2. Fold a large piece of aluminum foil into a bowl, and add to it the chopped garlic, cherry tomatoes, 1 tablespoon of oil, 1/4 teaspoon of salt, and 1/4 teaspoon of pepper. Lightly toss the ingredients of the foil bowl, before folding and sealing the edges.

3. Arrange the chicken kababs on the preheated grill, along with the foil pouch. Grill for 8-10 minutes, occasionally turning the kebabs and shaking the pouch to prevent burning, until the chicken is properly cooked. Use a basting brush to coat the kebabs with 1 tablespoon of lemon juice, before transferring the chicken to a plate, along with the aluminum foil pouch.

4. In a large bowl, toss together the dill, spring onions, lettuce, remaining oil and lemon juice, and 1/4 teaspoon each of salt and pepper.

5. Serve the chicken kebabs and roasted tomatoes on a bed of tossed salad, with lemon wedges on the side.

Per Serving:
Calories: 245, Fat: 13g, Protein: 25g, Carbohydrates: 8g, Fiber: 3g, Net Carbohydrates: 5g

QUICK & EASY CHICKEN CURRY

COOK TIME: 15 MINS | MAKES: 4 SERVINGS

INGREDIENTS:

- 1 tsp. ground turmeric
- 2 tsp. cayenne pepper
- 1 tbsp. garam masala
- 1 tbsp. ground cumin
- 1 tbsp. ground cilantro seeds
- 1 tsp. Himalayan salt
- 1/2 tsp. freshly ground black pepper
- 1 1/2 lbs. boneless chicken breasts, skins removed, cubed
- 2 tbsp. extra-virgin olive oil
- 1 tsp. crushed garlic
- 2 tbsp. fresh ginger, grated
- 1/2 cup chopped onions
- 2 tbsp. butter
- 1 cup canned crushed tomatoes
- 1/4 cup fresh coriander leaves, chopped (for garnish)
- 1 lime, quartered, for serving

DIRECTIONS:

1. In a large bowl, mix together the turmeric, cayenne pepper, masala, cumin, cilantro seeds, salt, and pepper. Add the chicken cubes, and toss to coat. Set aside while you prepare the rest of the curry.

2. In a large frying pan over medium-high heat, heat the olive oil. When the oil is nice and hot, fry the garlic, ginger, and onions for 2 minutes, allowing the flavors to meld. Scrape the chicken into the pan, and fry for 5 minutes while stirring, until the chicken is properly cooked.

3. Stir in the butter and tomatoes for 5 minutes. The sauce should thicken until it can coat the back of a wooden spoon.

4. Serve the curry garnished with the fresh coriander leaves, and with lime wedges on the side.

Quick Tip:
Any leftovers can be refrigerated in an airtight container for no more than 5 days, or frozen for 3 months.

Per Serving:
Calories: 315, Fat: 17g, Protein: 33g, Carbohydrates: 5g, Fiber: 1g, Net Carbohydrates: 4g

OVEN ROASTED CORIANDER & LIME CHICKEN

COOK TIME: 1 HOUR 20 MINS | MAKES: 6 SERVINGS

INGREDIENTS:

- 1 tsp. Himalayan salt
- 1 tsp. ground cumin
- 1 tsp. dried oregano
- 2 tbsp. fresh ginger, peeled and chopped
- 1 jalapeño chili, sliced
- 5 whole garlic cloves
- 3 tbsp. apple cider vinegar
- 1/4 cup freshly squeezed lime juice
- 1/3 cup soy sauce
- 1/2 cup extra-virgin olive oil
- 1/4 cup packed fresh tarragon leaves
- 1 cup packed fresh mint leaves
- 1 cup packed fresh coriander leaves
- 3 lbs. assorted chicken pieces, such as drumsticks and thighs
- 1/3 cup mayonnaise

DIRECTIONS:

1. Place the salt, cumin, oregano, ginger, chili, garlic, apple cider vinegar, lime juice, soy sauce, olive oil, tarragon, mint, and coriander in a high-powered food processor, and pulse on high until you have a lump-free paste. Scrape 3/4 cup of the mixture into an airtight container, and chill. Transfer the remainder of the marinade to a large, sealable plastic bag, and add the assorted chicken pieces. Seal the bag, and shake to distribute the marinade. Chill the bag overnight, or for a minimum of 5 hours.

2. Set the oven to preheat to 375°F, with the wire rack in the center of the oven. Fit a wire rack over a baking sheet covered in aluminum foil. Arrange the marinated chicken pieces on the rack, and discard the rest of the marinade. Bake the chicken in the oven for 30 minutes, then raise the temperature to 450°F, and continue to cook for 15-20 minutes, or until the chicken is nicely browned and properly cooked.

3. Remove the reserved marinade from the fridge, and whisk in the mayonnaise. Drizzle the sauce over the chicken when ready to serve.

Per Serving:
Calories: 500, Fat: 39g, Protein: 32g, Carbohydrates: 4g, Fiber: 1g, Net Carbohydrates: 3g

THREE CHEESE BUFFALO BAKE

COOK TIME: 25-30 MINS | MAKES: 6 SERVINGS

INGREDIENTS:

- 1/3 cup ranch dressing
- 1/3 cup buffalo wing sauce
- 1/3 cup sour cream
- 8 oz. cream cheese, softened
- 2 cups cheddar cheese, grated (divided)
- 1 tsp. garlic powder
- 2 tbsp. dried minced onion
- 2/3 cup celery, chopped
- 4 cups shredded cooked chicken
- 12 oz. frozen cauliflower florets, cooked and drained
- 1 cup mozzarella cheese, grated
- 1/2 cup cooked bacon pieces
- 1/4 cup parmesan cheese, for garnish

DIRECTIONS:

1. Grease a large casserole dish, and set the oven to preheat to 350°F, with the wire rack in the center of the oven.

2. Place the ranch dressing, buffalo wing sauce, sour cream, and cream cheese in a large mixing bowl, and whisk until you have a smooth sauce. Gently fold in 1 cup of cheddar, the garlic powder, dried minced onion, celery, and cooked chicken.

3. Place the cooked cauliflower in the center of a clean kitchen towel, and press as much moisture from the florets as you can. Slice the florets into bite-sized pieces before adding them to the bowl of chicken. Stir until all the ingredients are properly combined.

4. Scrape the chicken mixture into the prepared casserole dish, and top with the remaining cheddar. Sprinkle the mozzarella over the cheddar in an even layer, and top with the cooked bacon pieces.

5. Bake the dish in the oven for 25-30 minutes, or until the cheese is bubbling and lightly toasted on top.

6. Garnish the dish with parmesan cheese before serving hot.

Quick Tip:
Any leftovers can be refrigerated in an airtight container for no more than 4 days.

Per Serving:
Calories: 588, Fat: 37.2g, Protein: 33.1g, Carbohydrates: 4.7g, Fiber: 1.9g, Net Carbohydrates: 2.8g

SHERRY-BASED CREAMY CHICKEN & SAUCE

COOK TIME: 18 MINS | MAKES: 4 SERVINGS

INGREDIENTS:

- 6 tbsp. salted butter
- 1/4 cup onions, chopped
- 1/3 cup green bell peppers, chopped
- 1/3 cup celery, chopped
- 8 oz. button mushrooms, sliced
- 1 tbsp. powdered chicken bone broth
- 1 oz. jarred diced pimentos, drained
- 1/4 cup cream cheese
- 1/2 cup chicken stock
- 1 cup heavy cream
- 2 tbsp. cooking sherry
- Yolks of 2 large free-range eggs, beaten
- 1/4 tsp. Himalayan salt
- 1/8 tsp. freshly ground black pepper
- 5 cups shredded cooked chicken

DIRECTIONS:

1. In a large frying pan over medium heat, melt the butter. When the butter has melted, raise the temperature to medium-high, and fry the onions, bell peppers, celery, and mushrooms for 5-7 minutes, or until the mushrooms darken in color.

2. Lower the heat to medium-low, and stir in the bone broth, pimentos, cream cheese, chicken stock, and heavy cream, until the cream cheese has melted. Stir the sauce while simmering for 6-8 minutes, or until the sauce has reduced by half. Transfer the pan to a wooden chopping board, and stir in the sherry.

3. In a small glass bowl, whisk the egg yolks with 3 tablespoons of the sauce from the pan. Gradually pour the egg yolks into the hot pan while whisking.

4. Stir in the salt, pepper, and chicken until thoroughly incorporated. If you did not heat the chicken in the microwave, return the pan to low heat, and stir until the chicken is heated through. Keep an eye on the temperature, as you do not want the eggs to keep on cooking.

5. Serve the dish hot.

Per Serving:
Calories: 643, Fat: 56g, Protein: 32g, Carbohydrates: 5.4g, Fiber: 0.7g, Net Carbohydrates: 4.7g

CHICKEN CHOP WOW!

COOK TIME: 15 MINS | MAKES: 4 SERVINGS

INGREDIENTS:

- 1 tsp. toasted sesame oil
- 2 tbsp. extra-virgin olive oil
- 2 tsp. crushed garlic
- 1 lb. boneless chicken breasts, skins removed, thinly sliced
- 1 red bell pepper, thinly sliced into strips
- 1 cup celery stalks, thinly sliced
- 3 cups Bok choy, chopped, with leaves and stems separated
- 1/2 cup spring onions, sliced
- 1/2 cup canned bean sprouts, drained
- 1/2 tsp. xanthan gum
- 1 tbsp. no-sugar-added fish sauce
- 1 tbsp. coconut aminos
- 1/2 cup filtered water

DIRECTIONS:

1. In a large frying pan over medium-high heat, heat the sesame and olive oil. When the oil is nice and hot, fry the garlic for 1 minute, until the flavor is released. Add the chicken, and fry while stirring for 2-3 minutes, until evenly browned.

2. Add the peppers, celery, and Bok choy stems, frying for 3-5 minutes, or until the Bok choy stems are no longer opaque.

3. Stir in the Bok choy leaves, spring onions, and bean sprouts.

4. In a small glass bowl, whisk together the xanthan gum, fish sauce, coconut aminos, and water. Gradually stir the mixture into the pan, and simmer while stirring for 5 minutes, or until the sauce begins to thicken.

5. Scrape the contents of the pan onto a serving platter, and serve hot.

Quick Tip:
Any leftovers can be refrigerated in an airtight container for no more than 5 days, or frozen in an airtight container for no more than 3 months.

Per Serving:
Calories: 228, Fat: 11g, Protein: 24g, Carbohydrates: 6g, Fiber: 2g, Net Carbohydrates: 4g

DECADENT CHICKEN CURRY WITH COCONUT MILK

COOK TIME: 17 MINS | MAKES: 6 SERVINGS

INGREDIENTS:

- 1/4 tsp. freshly ground black pepper
- 1/2 tsp. ground cardamom
- 1/2 tsp. red chili flakes
- 1 tsp. turmeric powder
- 1 1/2 tsp. Himalayan salt
- 2 tsp. garam masala
- 1 tbsp. ground cumin
- 1 tbsp. ground cilantro seeds
- 2 tbsp. fresh ginger, peeled and grated
- 4 whole garlic cloves, peeled
- 1 cup onions, chopped
- 2 tbsp. extra-virgin olive oil
- 1/4 cup butter
- 1/2 cup tomatoes, chopped
- 1 1/2 lbs. chicken breasts, skins removed, cubed
- 1 cup chicken broth
- 1 cup canned coconut milk
- 1/4 cup shelled raw pumpkin seeds
- 1/4 cup fresh coriander leaves, chopped

DIRECTIONS:

1. In a high-powered blender, pulse the black pepper, cardamom, chili flakes, turmeric, salt, masala, cumin, cilantro seeds, ginger, garlic, onions, and olive oil on high, until you have a paste that is almost smooth, but still has a few lumps.

2. Scrape the paste into a large frying pan, and heat over medium heat for 2 minutes, continuously stirring until the flavors meld. Add the butter, tomatoes, and chicken cubes to the pan of spices. Stir and fry the chicken for about 5 minutes, or until it is nicely browned and properly cooked. Once the chicken is cooked, stir in the broth and coconut milk, using a wooden spoon to deglaze the pan, scraping up any bits of food that may have stuck to the bottom while cooking.

3. When the sauce begins to boil, reduce the heat to low, and simmer for 10 minutes, stirring at regular intervals to prevent burning, until the sauce has thickened and reduced by half.

4. Serve the curry hot, garnished with pumpkin seeds and fresh coriander leaves.

Quick Tip:
Any leftover curry can be refrigerated in an airtight container for no more than 5 days, or frozen in an airtight container for no more than 3 months.

Per Serving:
Calories: 319, Fat: 24g, Protein: 17g, Carbohydrates: 6g, Fiber: 1g, Net Carbohydrates: 5g

SPICY MEXICAN CHICKEN RELLENOS

COOK TIME: 30-40 MINS | MAKES: 8 SERVINGS

INGREDIENTS:

- 4 cups cooked chicken, chopped
- 7 oz. canned whole green chilies, chopped
- 2 tbsp. dried minced onion
- 1/2 cup Cotija cheese, grated or crumbled
- 2 cups Monterey Jack cheese, grated
- 2 cups mozzarella cheese, grated
- 1/4 tsp. Himalayan salt
- 1/2 tsp. baking powder
- 1/2 tsp. garlic powder
- 2 large free-range eggs
- 3/4 cup heavy cream
- Fresh coriander leaves, chopped (for garnish)
- Sour cream (for garnish)
- Diced avocado (for garnish)
- Prepared enchilada sauce (for garnish)

DIRECTIONS:

1. Set the oven to preheat to 350°F, with the wire rack in the center of the oven.

2. Place 2 cups of shredded chicken in the bottom of a large casserole dish, spreading it out in an even layer. Top the chicken with half of the green chilies and 1 tablespoon of the dried onions. Sprinkle half of the Cotija cheese over the onions, followed by half of the Monterey Jack and half of the mozzarella. Repeat the process with the remaining chicken, chilies, onions, Cotija, Monterey Jack, and mozzarella.

3. In a medium-sized mixing bowl, whisk together the salt, baking powder, garlic powder, eggs, and cream until properly combined. Carefully pour the beaten mixture over everything in the casserole dish, taking care not to disturb the layers. Use a sharp knife to cut small slits in the layers to ensure that the cream mixture soaks through everything.

4. Place the dish in the oven for 30-40 minutes, or until the cream mixture is no longer runny, and the cheese on top is bubbling and lightly toasted.

5. Allow the dish to cool on the counter for 10-15 minutes, before slicing and serving with 1 or more of the garnish options. Get creative for a flavor-packed dish!

Quick Tip:
Any leftovers can be refrigerated in an airtight container for no more than 4 days.

Per Serving:
Calories: 499, Fat: 32.7g, Protein: 33.4g, Carbohydrates: 4.1g, Fiber: 0.7g, Net Carbohydrates: 3.4g

OVEN CHICKEN PARMIGIANA

COOK TIME: 30-40 MINS | MAKES: 8 SERVINGS

INGREDIENTS:

- 2 lbs. chicken breast tenderloins, patted dry
- Himalayan salt
- Freshly ground black pepper
- 1 tsp. garlic powder
- 1 1/2 tsp. Italian seasoning (divided)
- 1/3 cup mayonnaise
- 1/2 cup pork rind dust
- 1/2 cup parmesan cheese, grated
- 14.5 oz. prepared no-sugar-added marinara sauce
- 2 cups mozzarella cheese, grated

DIRECTIONS:

1. Cover a large, rimmed baking pan with greaseproof paper, and set the oven to preheat to 350°F, with the wire rack in the center of the oven.

2. Place the chicken tenderloins on the prepared baking pan, and season with a pinch of salt and pepper, the garlic powder, and 1/2 teaspoon of Italian seasoning. Use clean hands to massage the spices into the chicken. Spread the mayonnaise on top of the chicken, and sprinkle with the pork rind dust and parmesan.

3. Place the pan in the oven for 20-25 minutes, or until the chicken is fork-tender, and the cheese is lightly toasted.

4. Remove the pan from the oven, and place a dollop of marinara sauce onto each tenderloin. Season the sauce with the final teaspoon of Italian seasoning before sprinkling the mozzarella cheese over the top. Place the tray back in the oven for 10-15 minutes, or until the cheese is melted and nicely toasted.

5. Plate the chicken immediately, and serve.

Quick Tip:
Any leftovers can be refrigerated in an airtight container for no more than 5 days.

Per Serving:
Calories: 285, Fat: 22g, Protein: 32.1g, Carbohydrates: 3.2g, Fiber: 0.5g, Net Carbohydrates: 2.7g

CAULIFLOWER ARROZ CON POLLO

COOK TIME: 30 MINS | MAKES: 6 SERVINGS

INGREDIENTS:

- 1/2 tsp. turmeric powder
- 3/4 tsp. freshly ground black pepper (divided)
- 1/2 tsp. dried thyme leaves
- 1 tsp. onion powder
- 1 tsp. ground cilantro seeds
- 1 tsp. garlic powder
- 1 tsp. dried oregano leaves
- 2 tsp. sweet smoked paprika
- 3 tsp. Himalayan salt (divided)
- 1 tbsp. ground cumin
- 6 bone-in, skin-on chicken thighs
- 3 tbsp. extra-virgin avocado oil
- 1 tsp. crushed garlic
- 1/4 cup any color sweet peppers, chopped
- 1/3 cup onions, chopped
- 4 cups riced cauliflower
- 1 tsp. capers, drained
- 10 pimento-stuffed olives, halved
- 1/2 cup canned diced tomatoes
- 1/4 cup fresh coriander leaves, chopped (for garnish)
- 1 lime, sliced into wedges, for serving

DIRECTIONS:

1. In a small glass bowl, whisk together the turmeric, 1/2 teaspoon of pepper, thyme, onion powder, cilantro seeds, garlic powder, oregano, paprika, 2 teaspoons of salt, and cumin. Place the chicken thighs on a clean chopping board, and massage the spice mixture into the chicken with clean hands.

2. In a large frying pan over medium heat, heat the oil. When the oil is nice and hot, fry the chicken for 5 minutes per side, or just until the skin is nicely seared all over. Transfer the seared thighs to a paper-towel-lined plate, and set aside.

3. With the pan still over medium heat, fry the garlic, sweet peppers, and onions for about 1 minute, or until the peppers and onions are fork-tender. Stir in the riced cauliflower, and the remaining pepper and salt. Fry the cauliflower, along with the peppers and onions, for about 5 minutes. Stir in the capers, olives, and diced tomatoes. Nestle the chicken thighs in the sauce, and simmer the pan uncovered for about 10 minutes, or until the sauce thickens, and the chicken is cooked all the way through.

4. Serve the chicken and sauce garnished with coriander leaves, and with lime wedges on the side.

Quick Tip:
Any leftovers can be refrigerated in an airtight container for no more than 5 days, or frozen for no more than 3 months.

Per Serving:
Calories: 451, Fat: 30g, Protein: 36g, Carbohydrates: 6g, Fiber: 2g, Net Carbohydrates: 4g

SHREDDED CORDON BLEU-STYLE CHICKEN

COOK TIME: 40-45 MINS | MAKES: 8 SERVINGS

INGREDIENTS:

- 8 slices smoked ham, chopped
- 4 cups cooked chicken, shredded
- 2 cups mozzarella cheese, shredded
- 1 tsp. Worcestershire sauce
- 1 tbsp. French mustard
- 1 1/2 cups heavy cream
- 2 tsp. powdered chicken bone broth
- 2 tbsp. salted butter, at room temperature
- 1/4 cup parmesan cheese, grated
- 1/2 cup pork rind dust
- Fresh parsley, chopped (for garnish)

DIRECTIONS:

1. Grease a large casserole dish, and set the oven to preheat to 350°F, with the wire rack in the center of the oven.

2. Place the chopped ham in the bottom of the prepared baking dish in an even layer, and top with the shredded chicken. Sprinkle half of the mozzarella over the chicken.

3. Whisk the Worcestershire sauce, mustard, heavy cream, and chicken bone broth together in a medium-sized bowl.

4. When the bone broth is fully incorporated into the cream, pour the spiced cream over everything in the casserole dish, and top the dish with the final cup of mozzarella.

5. In a small bowl, use your fingers to work the butter, parmesan, and pork rind dust into a mixture that resembles damp sand. Crumble the mixture over the casserole dish in an even layer.

6. Place the dish in the oven for 40-45 minutes, until the cheese starts bubbling and the top is nicely browned. Allow the dish to cool on the counter for 10-15 minutes before garnishing with fresh parsley, and serving.

Quick Tip:
Any leftovers can be refrigerated in an airtight container for no more than 4 days.

Per Serving:
Calories: 385, Fat: 32.1g, Protein: 29.1g, Carbohydrates: 3.6g, Fiber: 0.4g, Net Carbohydrates: 3.2g

KETO-FRIENDLY BAKED ENCHILADAS

COOK TIME: 45 MINS | MAKES: 6 SERVINGS

INGREDIENTS:

- 1 tsp. corn extract
- 1 tbsp. taco seasoning
- 1/4 cup cream cheese, softened
- 1/2 cup sour cream
- 10 oz. canned mild red enchilada sauce
- 2 cups mozzarella cheese, grated (divided)
- 2 tbsp. dried minced onion
- 2 tbsp. seeded and chopped jalapeño peppers
- 4 oz. canned diced green chilies
- 1 1/2 cups zucchini, finely chopped
- 2 cups cooked ground beef, crumbled and drained
- 3 cups cooked chicken, chopped
- 1 cup cheddar cheese, grated
- 1/4 cup Kalamata olives, seeded and halved
- Fresh coriander leaves, chopped (for garnish)

DIRECTIONS:

1. Grease a large casserole dish, and set the oven to preheat to 350°F, with the wire rack in the center of the oven.

2. Place the corn extract, taco seasoning, cream cheese, sour cream, and enchilada sauce in a large mixing bowl, and stir until all of the ingredients are properly combined. Stir in 1 1/2 cups of the mozzarella, the dried onion, jalapeños, green chilies, zucchini, ground beef, and chicken. Scrape the mixture into the prepared casserole dish in an even layer. Sprinkle the remaining mozzarella over the mixture, followed by the cheddar. Strew the olives over the cheese layers.

3. Cover the casserole dish in aluminum foil, and place it in the oven for 35-45 minutes, or until the zucchini is fork-tender and the cheese has melted. Discard the foil before returning the dish to the oven for 10-15 minutes, or until the top is lightly toasted.

4. Allow the dish to cool on the counter for a few minutes before garnishing with the fresh coriander leaves, and serving warm.

Quick Tip:
Any leftovers can be refrigerated in an airtight container for no more than 5 days.

Per Serving:
Calories: 575, Fat: 34.3g, Protein: 34.1g, Carbohydrates: 5.9g, Fiber: 2.1g, Net Carbohydrates: 3.8g

MILDLY SWEET BUTTER CHICKEN

COOK TIME: 25 MINS | MAKES: 6 SERVINGS

INGREDIENTS:

- 1/2 cup butter
- 2 lbs. boneless chicken breasts, skins removed, cubed
- 1 tsp. Himalayan salt
- 1/4 tsp. freshly ground black pepper
- 1/4 tsp. ground cinnamon
- 1/2 tsp. ground cardamom
- 1 tsp. ground cilantro seeds
- 2 tsp. sweet smoked paprika
- 1 tbsp. garam masala
- 1 tbsp. fresh ginger, peeled and minced
- 2 tbsp. tomato paste
- 1 tsp. crushed garlic
- 1/3 cup onions, chopped
- 1 tbsp. freshly squeezed lime juice
- 1 tbsp. coconut aminos
- 1 cup canned coconut milk
- 1/4 cup fresh coriander leaves, chopped (for garnish)
- 1 lime, cut into 6 wedges

DIRECTIONS:

1. In a large frying pan over medium-high heat, melt the butter. When the butter is bubbling, add the chicken, salt, and pepper, and fry for about 5 minutes, or until the chicken is nicely browned. Scrape the chicken onto a plate, before returning the pan to the heat.

2. With the heat on medium, add the cinnamon, cardamom, cilantro seeds, paprika, masala, ginger, tomato paste, garlic, and onions to the pan. Fry the spices and onions for about 2 minutes, allowing the flavors to meld. Scrape the chicken back into the pan, and fry while stirring for another 3 minutes, until the chicken is evenly coated in the spices.

3. Stir in the lime juice, coconut aminos, and coconut milk. Reduce the heat to low, and allow the sauce to simmer uncovered for 15 minutes, stirring at regular intervals, until the sauce has reduced and thickened.

4. Garnish the chicken with fresh coriander leaves, and serve with the lime wedges on the side.

Quick Tip:
Any leftovers can be refrigerated in an airtight container for no more than 5 days, or frozen for no more than 3 months.

Per Serving:
Calories: 375, Fat: 25g, Protein: 30g, Carbohydrates: 5g, Fiber: 1g, Net Carbohydrates: 4g

EASY LEMON & BUTTER CHICKEN

COOK TIME: 15 MINS | MAKES: 6 SERVINGS

INGREDIENTS:

- 1/3 cup mayonnaise
- 6 oz. chicken cutlets
- 1 tsp. Himalayan salt
- 1/4 tsp. freshly ground black pepper
- 1/4 tsp. garlic powder
- 1 tsp. lemon zest, finely grated
- 2 tbsp. coconut flour
- 1/3 cup sun-flour
- 2 tbsp. sunflower oil
- 2 tbsp. freshly squeezed lemon juice
- 1/4 cup butter
- 2 tbsp. fresh parsley, chopped (for garnish)
- 1 lemon, sliced into 6 wedges (for serving)

DIRECTIONS:

1. In a medium-sized mixing bowl, combine the mayonnaise and chicken, stirring until the chicken is evenly coated.

2. In a medium-sized bowl, whisk together the salt, pepper, garlic powder, lemon zest, coconut flour, and sun-flour. Dip the chicken in the bowl of flour, ensuring the mixture adheres to the mayonnaise in an even layer.

3. In a large frying pan over medium heat, heat the sunflower oil. When the oil is nice and hot, working in batches of 3 cutlets, fry the chicken for about 3 minutes per side, or until the chicken is properly cooked and nicely browned on all sides. Use tongs to transfer the cooked chicken to a serving platter. Wipe any bits of charred meat from the pan with greaseproof paper.

4. Stir in the lemon juice and butter for about 2 minutes, or just until the butter has melted and the lemon juice is properly incorporated. The sauce should thicken once the butter has melted.

5. Immediately pour the hot sauce over the cooked chicken. Garnish with fresh parsley leaves, and serve with the lemon wedges on the side.

Quick Tip:
Any leftovers can be refrigerated in an airtight container for no more than 5 days.

Per Serving:
Calories: 400, Fat: 17g, Protein: 41g, Carbohydrates: 3g, Fiber: 2g, Net Carbohydrates: 1g

BEEF, LAMB & PORK

RUSSIAN PORK STEW

COOK TIME: 20 MINS | MAKES: 4 SERVINGS

INGREDIENTS:

- 1 lb. pork tenderloin, sliced into thin strips
- Himalayan salt
- Freshly ground black pepper
- 2 tbsp. ghee (divided)
- 2 whole garlic cloves, minced
- 1 small onion, chopped
- 1 cup coconut milk
- 1 tbsp. French mustard
- 1 tbsp. freshly squeezed lemon juice
- 1 cup chicken stock
- 3 cups button mushrooms, sliced
- 2 tbsp. fresh parsley, chopped (extra for garnish)
- 1 lb. asparagus spears

DIRECTIONS:

1. Place the pork strips in a large mixing bowl, and season with a large pinch of salt and pepper. In a large saucepan over high heat, melt 1 tablespoon of the ghee. When the ghee is nice and hot, fry the seasoned pork strips for a few minutes, until evenly browned on all sides. You do not want to overcrowd the pan, so work in batches if necessary. Transfer the cooked strips to a paper-towel-lined plate when done.

2. Add the rest of the ghee to the pan, and when it has melted, fry the garlic and onions for about 3 minutes, or until the flavors meld and the onions soften.

3. Stir in the coconut milk, mustard, lemon juice, chicken stock, and button mushrooms. Bring the sauce to a boil, then stir for 5 minutes, or until the sauce begins to thicken. Transfer the pot to a wooden chopping board, taste the sauce, and season with extra salt and pepper to taste, if desired. Add the pork, and stir to combine.

4. Bring a large pot of salted water to a rolling boil, and add in the asparagus spears. Boil the spears for 2-3 minutes, until tender but still crisp. Use a slotted spoon to transfer the asparagus to a colander set over the sink.

5. Serve the pork stew with the asparagus spears on the side, garnished with extra parsley if desired.

Per Serving:
Calories: 556, Fat: 42.8g, Protein: 32.5g, Carbohydrates: 10.7g, Fiber: 3.7g, Net Carbohydrates: 7g

SIMPLE MEATBALLS & ZUCCHINI NOODLES

COOK TIME: 15 MINS | MAKES: 4 SERVINGS

INGREDIENTS:

- 2 tbsp. extra-virgin avocado oil
- 1 tsp. Himalayan salt
- 1/4 tsp. freshly ground black pepper
- 1/2 tsp. onion powder
- 1/2 tsp. garlic powder
- 1/2 tsp. dried and crushed oregano leaves
- 1/4 cup fresh parsley, finely chopped
- 1/4 cup mayonnaise
- 1/4 cup shelled hemp seeds
- 1 lb. ground beef
- 6 cups zucchini noodles
- 1 1/2 cups marinara sauce
- Fresh basil sprigs for garnish

DIRECTIONS:

1. Grease a large, rimmed baking tray with the avocado oil, and set the oven to preheat to 400°F, with the wire rack in the center of the oven.

2. In a large mixing bowl, use clean hands to combine the salt, pepper, onion powder, garlic powder, oregano, parsley, mayonnaise, hemp seeds, and ground beef. Shape the mixture into 12 balls of roughly the same size. Place each ball on the prepared baking tray, and roll it around in the oil. When all 12 balls are evenly coated in oil, space them out evenly on half of the tray. Place the tray in the oven for 10 minutes

3. Remove the tray from the oven and add the zucchini noodles. Toss the noodles a few times in the sauce from the pan, until evenly coated. Drizzle the marinara sauce over all of the noodles.

4. Place the tray back in the oven for 5-7 minutes, or until the zucchini noodles are cooked but still crisp.

5. Remove the tray from the oven, and use tongs to transfer the cooked meatballs to a serving platter. Carefully tilt the tray of noodles over a bowl, while holding the noodles back with a large spoon, to drain any excess fluids.

6. Serve the cooked meatballs on a bed of zucchini noodles, garnished with fresh basil sprigs.

Quick Tip:
Any leftovers can be refrigerated in an airtight container for no more than 5 days.

Per Serving:
Calories: 501, Fat: 40g, Protein: 25g, Carbohydrates: 9g, Fiber: 4g, Net Carbohydrates: 5g

SPICY TURKEY LETTUCE BOWLS

COOK TIME: 15 MINS | MAKES: 4 SERVINGS

INGREDIENTS:

- 2 tbsp. ghee
- 1 large green pepper, sliced
- 1 small onion, chopped
- 1 tbsp. balsamic vinegar
- 1 tsp. French mustard
- 1 tsp. cayenne pepper
- 1 lb. ground turkey
- 9.5 oz. heirloom tomatoes, chopped
- 1/4 cup no-sugar-added tomato paste
- Himalayan salt
- Freshly ground black pepper
- 2 medium heads of iceberg lettuce
- 1/4 cup extra-virgin olive oil
- 2 medium scallions, sliced

DIRECTIONS:

1. In a large frying pan over medium-high heat, melt the ghee. When the ghee is nice and hot, fry the peppers and onions for 2-3 minutes, or until they begin to soften. Stir in the vinegar, mustard, cayenne pepper, and ground turkey. Cook the turkey while stirring for 7-8 minutes, until properly cooked.

2. Stir in the chopped tomatoes and tomato paste. When the sauce starts to boil, lower the heat to medium, and simmer for 8-10 minutes, or until the sauce thickens to coat the back of a wooden spoon. Taste the sauce, and add a pinch of salt and pepper as needed. Transfer the pan to a wooden chopping board, and set aside for 5 minutes.

3. To build your bowls, place 2 or more leaves of lettuce in a serving bowl. Spoon the cooked turkey onto the leaves, and drizzle with a bit of olive oil before garnishing with sliced scallions. Repeat with the other bowls, and serve.

Quick Tip:
Any leftover ground turkey can be refrigerated in an airtight container for no more than 3 days, or frozen for no more than 3 months. The lettuce should not be stored along with the mince, use fresh, crisp lettuce each time.

Per Serving:
Calories: 462, Fat: 37.5g, Protein: 23.4g, Carbohydrates: 10.8g, Fiber: 3.6g, Net Carbohydrates: 7.2g

KETO-STYLE STIR-FRY

COOK TIME: 10 MINS | MAKES: 4 SERVINGS

INGREDIENTS:

- 14 oz. shirataki noodles, drained
- 4 tbsp. ghee (divided)
- 1 lb. sirloin steak, sliced into strips
- Himalayan salt
- Freshly ground black pepper
- 1 tbsp. freshly peeled ginger, grated
- 1 small chili pepper, diced
- 2 whole garlic cloves, diced
- 7.1 oz. mixed Asian mushrooms, sliced (shiitake, oyster, and enoki)
- 2 tbsp. fish sauce
- 2 tbsp. coconut aminos
- 2 medium green peppers, sliced
- 2 cups bean sprouts
- 2 tbsp. fresh coriander leaves, chopped
- 2 medium scallions, sliced
- 1 tbsp. toasted sesame oil
- 2 tbsp. freshly squeezed lime juice

DIRECTIONS:

1. Place the noodles in a colander over the sink, and rinse thoroughly with clean water. Cook the noodles in a pot of salted boiling water for 2-3 minutes, before straining once again through the colander.

2. In a large frying pan over medium-high heat, fry the noodles without any added oil or water for 1o minutes, tossing as you fry. Transfer the cooked noodles to a serving platter, and keep warm. Dry-frying the noodles will ensure the best texture.

3. In a large frying pan over medium-high heat, melt 2 tablespoons of the ghee. When the ghee is nice and hot, fry the beef strips with a large pinch of salt and pepper, until properly cooked. Use tongs to transfer the cooked beef into a bowl, and set aside.

4. In the same pan, melt 2 more tablespoons of ghee. When the ghee has melted, fry the ginger, chili, and garlic for 2-3 minutes, allowing the flavors to meld.

5. Scrape the mushrooms into the pan, and fry for 5 minutes before adding the fish sauce, coconut aminos, and sliced green peppers. Fry for an additional 3-5 minutes. Add the cooked beef and noodles to the pan, along with the bean sprouts, and fry for 1 minute, until everything is heated through.

6. Transfer the pan to a wooden chopping board, and stir in the coriander leaves, scallions, sesame oil, and lime juice.

7. Plate the stir-fry, and serve immediately.

Quick Tip:
Any leftovers can be refrigerated in an airtight container for no more than 3 days.

Per Serving:
Calories: 449, Fat: 32.9g, Protein: 28.9g, Carbohydrates: 11.8g, Fiber: 4g, Net Carbohydrates: 7.8g

CHEESY BURGER BAKED CASSEROLE

COOK TIME: 25-30 MINS | MAKES: 6 SERVINGS

INGREDIENTS:

- 2 large free-range eggs
- 3/4 cup cream cheese, softened
- 1/3 cup mozzarella cheese, grated
- 1/2 cup parmesan cheese, grated
- 2 cups strong cheddar cheese, grated
- 1/2 cup mayonnaise
- 1/2 tsp. garlic powder
- 1 tsp. Himalayan salt
- 1 tsp. baking powder
- 2 tsp. Worcestershire sauce
- 2 tbsp. dried minced onions
- 3/4 cup cooked bacon, diced
- 1 lb. cooked ground beef, crumbled and drained
- 1 heirloom tomato, sliced (for garnish)

DIRECTIONS:

1. Grease a large casserole dish, and set the oven to preheat to 375°F, with the wire rack in the center of the oven.

2. Place the eggs and cream cheese in a large mixing bowl, and beat until creamy. Stir in the mozzarella, parmesan, cheddar, and mayonnaise, until the ingredients come together. Stir in the garlic powder, salt, baking powder, Worcestershire sauce, dried minced onions, bacon, and beef, until all of the ingredients are properly combined.

3. Scrape the mixture into the prepared baking dish in an even layer. Place the dish in the oven for 25-30 minutes, or until the cheese is melted and nicely toasted.

4. Allow the dish to stand for 5-10 minutes on the counter before garnishing with the tomato slices, slicing, and serving.

Quick Tip:
Any leftovers can be refrigerated in an airtight container for no more than 4 days, or frozen for no more than 2 months.

Per Serving:
Calories: 667, Fat: 35g, Protein: 31g, Carbohydrates: 4.8g, Fiber: 2.4g, Net Carbohydrates: 2.4g

TRUFFLE BUTTER PORK CHOPS

COOK TIME: 15 MINS | MAKES: 4 SERVINGS

INGREDIENTS:

- 2 tbsp. extra-virgin avocado oil
- 4 bone-in pork chops, about 1-inch thick each
- Himalayan salt
- Freshly ground black pepper
- 1/2 tsp. fresh rosemary, chopped
- 12 oz. button mushrooms, thinly sliced
- 3 medium onions, chopped
- 2 tbsp. truffle butter
- 1/3 cup half-and-half

DIRECTIONS:

1. Heat the oil in a large frying pan over medium-high heat. When the oil is nice and hot, season the pork chops with 1/2 teaspoon each of salt and pepper, and fry for 3 minutes per side, or until just seared. Transfer the chops to a large plate, and tent to keep warm.

2. Lower the heat, and remove all but 1-2 tablespoons of the grease. Fry the rosemary, mushrooms, onions, and 1/8 teaspoon of salt for 5 minutes, stirring at regular intervals to prevent burning.

3. Stir in the truffle butter and half-and-half. When the butter has melted, return the pork chops to the pan, and fry simmer for 3-4 minutes per side, or until the pork is properly cooked.

4. Serve immediately.

Per Serving:
Calories: 400, Fat: 25g, Protein: 33g, Carbohydrates: 9g, Fiber: 1g, Net Carbohydrates: 8g

TANGY MUSTARD SALAD & PORK TENDERLOINS

COOK TIME: 35 MINS | MAKES: 4 SERVINGS

INGREDIENTS:

- 12 oz. green beans, trimmed
- Himalayan salt
- Extra-virgin olive oil
- 1 1/4 lbs. pork tenderloin
- Freshly ground black pepper
- 1 tsp. mayonnaise
- 1 small onion, finely chopped
- 2 tbsp. red wine vinegar
- 3 tbsp. French mustard
- 2 cups cherry tomatoes, halved
- 6 cups baby kale

DIRECTIONS:

1. Set the grill to preheat on medium, and line a large, rimmed baking tray with aluminum foil.

2. Place the beans in the center of the foil-lined tray, and toss with 1/4 teaspoon of salt and 1 teaspoon of oil, until the beans are evenly coated. Fold the foil over the beans, and seal the edges to create a pouch. Grill the beans covered for 20 minutes.

3. Season the pork tenderloin with 2 teaspoons of oil, and 1/2 teaspoon each of salt and pepper. Grill the tenderloin for 18-20 minutes, turning at regular intervals, until properly cooked. Let the tenderloin stand for 5 minutes on a wooden chopping board before slicing.

4. In a large bowl, whisk together 1 teaspoon of oil, 1/4 teaspoon of salt, the mayonnaise, onion, red wine vinegar, and mustard. Add the cherry tomatoes and baby kale, tossing until they are evenly coated.

5. Plate the grilled pork on a bed of grilled beans, with the coated salad on the side. Serve with extra mustard dressing from the bowl, if desired.

Per Serving:
Calories: 290, Fat: 13g, Protein: 32g, Carbohydrates: 11g, Fiber: 5g, Net Carbohydrates: 6g

RICH & TENDER BEEF CURRY

COOK TIME: 55 MINS | MAKES: 6 SERVINGS

INGREDIENTS:

- 2 tbsp. extra-virgin avocado oil
- 2 tsp. lime zest, finely grated
- 2 tsp. fresh ginger, peeled and minced
- 2 whole cloves garlic, minced
- 2 tsp. Himalayan salt
- 1/2 tsp. freshly ground black pepper
- 1 tsp. garam masala
- 2 tsp. turmeric powder
- 1 tbsp. ground cumin
- 2 tbsp. ground coriander seeds
- 3 lbs. stew beef, cut into 1-inch cubes
- 1 tbsp. balsamic vinegar
- 3/4 cup beef stock
- 1 tsp. habanero peppers, minced
- 1/2 cup tomatoes, diced
- 1 tsp. garam masala
- 2 tsp. coconut milk powder
- 1/3 cup sun-flour
- 1/4 cup fresh coriander leaves, chopped (for garnish)

DIRECTIONS:

1. Place the oil, lime zest, ginger, garlic, salt, pepper, masala, turmeric, cumin, and ground coriander seeds in a large mixing bowl, and whisk to combine. Add the beef cubes, and toss until they are evenly coated.

2. Set the dial of an instant pot to sauté. When the pot is hot, add half of the coated beef, and fry for 2-3 minutes, until evenly browned. Scrape the browned beef into a bowl, and brown the rest of the beef for 2-3 minutes. With all of the beef back in the pot, stir in the vinegar, stock, habanero peppers, and tomatoes. Seal the pot lid with the steam valve closed, and cook for 40 minutes on manual/high. Make sure to read the pot instructions on how to release the steam carefully, to avoid any nasty burns. Once the steam is released, transfer the cooked meat to a plate with a slotted spoon.

3. With the dial set back to sauté, whisk the masala, coconut milk powder, and sun-flour for 5-7 minutes, until the sauce thickens. Scrape the meat back into the pot, and stir to combine. Taste the sauce, and add extra salt, if desired.

4. Serve the curry garnished with fresh coriander leaves.

Quick Tip:
Any leftovers can be refrigerated in an airtight container for no more than 5 days, or frozen for no more than 3 months.

Per Serving:
Calories: 481, Fat: 35g, Protein: 43g, Carbohydrates: 3g, Fiber: 1g, Net Carbohydrates: 2g

OVEN-BAKED STEAK & VEG

COOK TIME: 20 MINS | MAKES: 4 SERVINGS

INGREDIENTS:

- 3 tbsp. extra-virgin olive oil
- 2 tsp. crushed garlic
- 1/2 cup red onions, sliced
- 1 cup poblano peppers, sliced
- 1 cup sweet peppers, sliced
- 1 tsp. Himalayan salt
- 1/2 tsp. freshly ground black pepper
- 1/2 tsp. garlic powder
- 1 tsp. cayenne pepper
- 1 tbsp. ground cumin
- 1 lb. beef sirloin, sliced into thin strips

DIRECTIONS:

1. Set the oven to preheat to 400°F, with the wire rack in the center of the oven.

2. On a large, rimmed baking sheet, toss the olive oil with the garlic, red onions, poblano peppers, and sweet peppers, until everything is evenly coated in oil.

3. In a large mixing bowl, whisk together the salt, pepper, garlic powder, cayenne pepper, and cumin. Add the sirloin strips, and toss to coat, or use a wooden spoon to stir until the meat strips are evenly coated in the spice mixture. Toss the seasoned steak with the vegetables on the baking sheet, and spread everything out in a single layer.

4. Place the sheet in the oven for 20 minutes, or until the beef is cooked, and the vegetables are fork-tender. Serve the beef and vegetables hot.

Quick Tip:
Any leftovers can be refrigerated in an airtight container for no more than 5 days.

Per Serving:
Calories: 266, Fat: 9g, Protein: 32g, Carbohydrates: 5g, Fiber: 1g, Net Carbohydrates: 4g

SWEET & TANGY GINGER BEEF

COOK TIME: 10 MINS | MAKES: 4 SERVINGS

INGREDIENTS:

- 1 tsp. toasted sesame oil
- 2 tbsp. extra-virgin olive oil
- 2 tsp. crushed garlic
- 1 tbsp. fresh ginger, grated
- 1 cup red bell peppers, sliced
- 1 cup broccoli florets
- 1/2 tsp. Himalayan salt
- 1/4 tsp. freshly ground black pepper
- 1 tsp. no-sugar-added fish sauce
- 1 tbsp. white vinegar
- 1 tbsp. coconut aminos
- 1 lb. boneless flank steak, thinly sliced
- 1/4 tsp. xanthan gum
- 1/4 cup filtered water
- 1 cup spring onions, green parts only, thinly sliced

DIRECTIONS:

1. In a large frying pan over medium-high heat, heat the olive oil and sesame oil. When the oil is nice and hot, fry the garlic and ginger for 1 minute, allowing the flavors to meld. Stir in the bell peppers and broccoli florets for 3 minutes, or until the broccoli becomes tender, and brightens in color.

2. Stir in the salt, pepper, fish sauce, vinegar, coconut aminos, and steak strips, frying for 2 minutes, or until the steak just begins to brown.

3. Stir in the xanthan gum and filtered water for 3 additional minutes, until the beef is cooked all the way through, and the sauce has thickened slightly. The broccoli should be soft when pierced with a fork.

4. Transfer the pan to a wooden chopping board, and stir in the spring onions.

5. Serve the beef hot.

Quick Tip:
Any leftovers can be refrigerated in an airtight container for no more than 5 days.

Per Serving:
Calories: 289, Fat: 14g, Protein: 33g, Carbohydrates: 6g, Fiber: 2g, Net Carbohydrates: 4g

OVEN-BAKED BACON & PATTIES

COOK TIME: 20-25 MINS | MAKES: 4 SERVINGS

INGREDIENTS:

- 1 tsp. Himalayan salt
- 1/4 tsp. freshly ground black pepper
- 1/2 tsp. garlic powder
- 1 1/2 lbs. ground beef
- 2 habanero peppers, sliced into rings
- 4 thick slices red onion
- 6 bacon slices, cut in half lengthwise
- 1/2 cup hot sauce

DIRECTIONS:

1. Set the oven to preheat to 425°F, with the wire rack in the center of the oven.

2. In a large mixing bowl, use clean hands to combine the salt, pepper, garlic powder, and ground beef. Form the mixture into 4 balls of roughly the same size, and press them down into 1-inch-thick patties. Place the patties on half of a large baking tray. Arrange the habanero slices, onion rings, and bacon strips on the other half of the pan.

3. Place the sheet in the oven for 20-25 minutes, or until the patties are done to your liking.

4. Plate the patties, and top with the roasted ingredients in equal amounts. Serve immediately, and enjoy!

Quick Tip:
Any leftovers can be refrigerated in an airtight container for no more than 5 days.

Per Serving:
Calories: 510, Fat: 39g, Protein: 36g, Carbohydrates: 4g, Fiber: 1g, Net Carbohydrates: 3g

PORK & EGGPLANT ROLL-UPS

COOK TIME: 35 MINS | MAKES: 5 SERVINGS

INGREDIENTS:

For the sauce:

- 1/2 tsp. Himalayan salt
- 1/4 tsp. freshly ground black pepper
- 1/4 tsp. garlic powder
- 1 tsp. dried onion flakes
- 1 tsp. unsweetened balsamic vinegar
- 1 tbsp. fresh mint leaves, chopped
- 2 tbsp. extra-virgin avocado oil
- 1 cup canned crushed tomatoes

For the filling:

- 1 tsp. Himalayan salt
- 1/4 tsp. freshly ground black pepper
- 1/4 tsp. allspice
- 1/2 tsp. cumin
- 1/2 tsp. ground coriander
- 1/2 tsp. garlic powder
- 1 tsp. garam masala
- 3 tbsp. pine nuts, roughly chopped
- 1 lb. ground pork

For the roll-ups:

- 4 long eggplants, sliced lengthwise into 1/4-inch-thick strips
- Pine nuts (for garnish)
- Fresh mint leaves, roughly chopped (for garnish)

DIRECTIONS:

1. Set the oven to preheat to 375°F, with the wire rack in the center of the oven.

2. In a large mixing bowl, whisk together the salt, pepper, garlic powder, onion flakes, vinegar, mint leaves, avocado oil, and crushed tomatoes. Scoop half of the sauce into a large baking dish, and set the rest aside for later.

3. In a separate large mixing bowl, use clean hands to combine the salt, pepper, allspice, cumin, coriander, garlic powder, masala, pine nuts, and ground pork.

4. Arrange the eggplant slices on a clean chopping board, and spread 1 tablespoon of the pork filling over each slice. Roll the slices up as tight as you can, like sushi rolls. Continue until all of the filing has been used up. There may be a few slices of eggplant left over, which can be discarded or used for another recipe. Place the rolled up eggplants upright in the baking dish with the sauce, and pour the reserved sauce over the roll-ups.

5. Place the dish in the oven for 35 minutes, or until the rolls are nicely toasted on top, and the pork is properly cooked.

6. Serve the roll-ups hot, garnished with pine nuts and fresh mint leaves.

Quick Tip:
Any leftovers can be refrigerated in an airtight container for no more than 5 days.

Per Serving:
Calories: 300, Fat: 19g, Protein: 19g, Carbohydrates: 9g, Fiber: 5g, Net Carbohydrates: 4g

BANGERS & CREAMY CAULIFLOWER MASH

COOK TIME: 20 MINS | MAKES: 4 SERVINGS

INGREDIENTS:

- 4 fresh pork sausages
- 1 tbsp. extra-virgin avocado oil
- 2 tbsp. butter
- 1 cup onions, sliced
- 1/2 tsp. Himalayan salt
- 1/4 tsp. freshly ground black pepper
- 1 tsp. red wine vinegar
- 1/3 cup chicken stock
- 1 batch garlic & chive cauliflower mash, hot
- 2 tbsp. fresh parsley, chopped (for garnish)

DIRECTIONS:

1. In a large frying pan over medium heat, fry the sausages for about 3 minutes per side, or until they are nicely browned on all sides, and properly cooked. Transfer the cooked sausages to a plate, and tent to keep warm.

2. With the pan still over medium heat, heat the avocado oil and butter, and fry the onions for about 7 minutes, or until they become a crispy brown around the edges. Stir in the salt, pepper, vinegar, and chicken stock. When the sauce begins to simmer, keep an eye on the heat, and simmer for 5 minutes, until the sauce thickens and reduces by half.

3. Use a sharp knife to halve the sausages lengthwise. Nestle the sausage halves in the sauce, and simmer while stirring, until heated through.

4. Place 1/2 cup of cauliflower mash on each plate, and top with 2 sausage halves and 2 tablespoons of gravy per plate. Serve hot, and enjoy garnished with fresh parsley leaves.

Quick Tip:
Any leftovers can be refrigerated in an airtight container for no more than 5 days.

Per Serving:
Calories: 510, Fat: 44g, Protein: 17g, Carbohydrates: 12g, Fiber: 4g, Net Carbohydrates: 8g

ALL-DAY PORK ROAST

COOK TIME: 6-7 HOURS | MAKES: 15 SERVINGS

INGREDIENTS:

- 1 tbsp. sweet smoked paprika
- 1 tbsp. onion powder
- 1 tbsp. ground cumin
- 2 tbsp. Himalayan salt
- 1 tbsp. freshly ground black pepper
- 1 tbsp. dried oregano leaves
- 2 tbsp. garlic powder
- 8 lbs. bone-in pork shoulder

DIRECTIONS:

1. Set the oven to preheat to 500°F, with the wire rack in the center of the oven.

2. In a small glass bowl, mix together the sweet smoked paprika, onion powder, cumin, salt, pepper, oregano, and garlic powder.

3. Place the pork shoulder in a large roasting pan, and use a sharp knife to cut a crisscross pattern over the surface of the meat, going deep into the fat layer. Sprinkle the spice mixture over the roast, and use clean hands to massage the spices into the meat. The fat layer should be facing up during roasting.

4. Place the pan in the oven for 20 minutes, uncovered. After 20 minutes, lower the temperature to 300°F, and roast the shoulder uncovered for 6 hours.

5. Remove the roast from the oven, and tent with aluminum foil for 30 minutes. After 30 minutes, slice the roast as desired, and serve.

Per Serving:
Calories: 275, Fat: 15g, Protein: 39g, Carbohydrates: 2g, Fiber: 0.5g, Net Carbohydrates: 1.5g

FIERY PORK VINDALOO

COOK TIME: 20 MINS | MAKES: 6 SERVINGS

INGREDIENTS:

- 3 tbsp. extra-virgin olive oil
- 3 whole cloves garlic, minced
- 1/3 cup onions, chopped
- 1/2 cup sweet peppers, chopped
- 3 bay leaves, torn
- 1/8 tsp. ground cloves
- 1/4 tsp. mustard powder
- 1/2 tsp. turmeric powder
- 1/2 tsp. ground cardamom
- 1 tsp. Himalayan salt
- 1 tsp. ground coriander seeds
- 1 tsp. ground cinnamon
- 1 tsp. ground ginger
- 2 tsp. cayenne pepper
- 1 tbsp. ground cumin
- 1 1/2 lbs. pork loin, sliced into bite-sized pieces
- 1 tbsp. coconut aminos
- 2 tbsp. unsweetened balsamic vinegar
- 1/2 cup filtered water
- 1/2 cup canned crushed tomatoes

DIRECTIONS:

1. In a medium-sized pot over medium heat, heat the olive oil. When the oil is nice and hot, fry the garlic, onions, and sweet peppers for 2-3 minutes, or until the onions begin to soften. Stir in the bay leaves, cloves, mustard, turmeric, cardamom, salt, coriander seeds, cinnamon, ginger, cayenne pepper, and cumin for 2 minutes, allowing the flavors to meld.

2. Scrape the sliced pork into the pot, and brown for 5 minutes, stirring at regular intervals to prevent burning. Stir in the coconut aminos, vinegar, water, and crushed tomatoes. Bring the sauce to a boil, before lowering the heat to maintain a gentle simmer for 10 minutes. The pork should be nice and soft when ready.

3. Discard the bay leaves, and serve the curry hot.

Quick Tip:
Any leftovers can be refrigerated in an airtight container for no more than 5 days, or frozen for no more than 3 months.

Per Serving:
Calories: 241, Fat: 10g, Protein: 27g, Carbohydrates: 5g, Fiber: 1g, Net Carbohydrates: 4g

LOADED GLAZED ONIONS

COOK TIME: 45 MINS | MAKES: 4 SERVINGS

INGREDIENTS:

- 4 medium red onions
- 1 lb. breakfast sausage
- 2 tsp. red wine vinegar glaze

DIRECTIONS:

1. Set the oven to preheat to 375°F, with the wire rack in the center of the oven.

2. Place the onions on a wooden chopping board, and slice half an inch off the top and bottom of each onion. Discard the outer skins. Use a sharp paring knife to slice a cross into the center of each onion, all the way to the bottom, taking care not to damage the 3 outer layers. Remove the inside layers of onion, until only the 3 outer layers remain.

3. Remove the sausage casings, and crumble the meat. Divide the meat between the 4 hollow onions, packing it in tightly.

4. Arrange the 4 stuffed onions in a small or medium roasting dish, and bake in the oven for 45 minutes, or until the meat is properly cooked and the onions are tender.

5. Plate the stuffed onions, and drizzle with the red wine vinegar glaze before serving.

Quick Tip:
Any leftovers can be refrigerated in an airtight container for no more than 5 days.

Per Serving:
Calories: 367, Fat: 30g, Protein: 17g, Carbohydrates: 6g, Fiber: 1g, Net Carbohydrates: 5g

MINI CHEESEBURGER MEATLOAVES

COOK TIME: 30 MINS | MAKES: 4 SERVINGS

INGREDIENTS:

- 8 thin bacon slices, partially cooked
- 1/4 tsp, Himalayan salt
- 1/2 tsp. freshly ground black pepper
- 1 tbsp. Worcestershire sauce
- 2 tbsp. dried minced onions
- 1/4 cup dill pickles, chopped
- 1/2 cup no-sugar-added tomato sauce (extra for glaze)
- 1 large free-range egg
- 1 cup mozzarella cheese, grated
- 1 lb. ground beef

DIRECTIONS:

1. Set the oven to preheat to 375°F, with the wire rack in the center of the oven, and grease 8 cups of a standard muffin tin.

2. Line the inside of each greased muffin cup with 1 strip of partially cooked bacon.

3. In a large mixing bowl, use clean hands to combine the salt, pepper, Worcestershire sauce, minced onions, dill pickles, tomato sauce, egg, cheese, and ground beef, until all of the ingredients come together.

4. Divide the meat mixture between the bacon-lined muffin cups, patting the meat down. Glaze the top of each mini meatloaf with extra tomato sauce.

5. Bake the meatloaves in the oven for 30 minutes, or until the meat is cooked all the way through.

6. Serve hot, 2 per plate.

Per Serving:
Calories: 548, Fat: 42.3g, Protein: 34.8g, Carbohydrates: 5.2g, Fiber: 0.4g, Net Carbohydrates: 4.8g

HARD-SEARED ROSEMARY STEAKS

COOK TIME: 27 MINS | MAKES: 2 SERVINGS

INGREDIENTS:

- 2 bone-in rib-eye steaks, 1 1/2-inches thick
- Himalayan salt
- Freshly ground black pepper
- 2 tbsp. salted butter
- 2 whole garlic cloves, crushed
- 2 sprigs fresh rosemary

DIRECTIONS:

1. Place the steaks on a wooden chopping board, and season both sides of each steak with salt and pepper to taste. Allow the steaks to sit on the chopping board for 30 minutes.

2. Cover a medium baking sheet with aluminum foil, and place a fitted wire rack over the sheet. Set the oven to preheat to 275°F, with the wire rack in the center of the oven.

3. Once the steaks have been standing at room temperature for 30 minutes, arrange them on the wire rack set over the tray, and bake in the oven for 25 minutes, or until they are done to your liking. Allow the steaks to rest once more at room temperature for 15 minutes.

4. In a large, cast-iron frying pan over medium heat, melt the butter. When the butter is sizzling hot, add the steaks to the pan, and sear for 1 minute. Turn the steaks, and add the garlic and rosemary to the butter in the pan, shaking the pan to spread the flavors. Spoon the hot butter over the steaks while you hard-sear the bottoms for 1 minute.

5. Plate the steaks with some of the garlic and butter spooned over the tops. Serve hot, and enjoy.

Per Serving:
Calories: 559, Fat: 46g, Protein: 32.8g, Carbohydrates: 3.9g, Fiber: 2.1g, Net Carbohydrates: 1.8g

LAMB & MINT MINI MEATLOAVES

COOK TIME: 20 MINS | MAKES: 4 SERVINGS

INGREDIENTS:

- Himalayan salt
- 1/2 cup fresh mint leaves, finely chopped
- 1/2 cup feta cheese, crumbled
- 1 1/4 lbs. ground lamb
- 1 tbsp. extra-virgin olive oil
- 1 cup pitted green olives
- 3 medium yellow squash, chopped
- 1 large leek, sliced

DIRECTIONS:

1. Set the oven to preheat to 450°F, with the wire rack in the center of the oven. Line a large, rimmed baking sheet with aluminum foil.

2. In a large mixing bowl, combine 1/4 teaspoon of salt with the mint leaves, feta, and lamb. Using clean hands, shape the mixture into 4 mini meatloaves of roughly the same size, and place each mini loaf on a corner of the prepared baking sheet.

3. In a separate mixing bowl, toss together the olive oil, 1/8 teaspoon of salt, olives, squash, and leeks, until all of the ingredients are evenly coated. Spread the coated vegetables out on the baking sheet between the mini meatloaves.

4. Place the sheet in the oven for 15-20 minutes, or until the mini meatloaves are cooked all the way through, and nicely browned on top. The vegetables should be fork-tender.

5. Serve the mini meatloaves alongside the roasted vegetables.

Per Serving:
Calories: 415, Fat: 28g, Protein: 30g, Carbohydrates: 12g, Fiber: 4g, Net Carbohydrates: 8g

SOUPS & STEWS

CHEESY BROCCOLI SOUP

COOK TIME: 20 MINS | MAKES: 4 SERVINGS

INGREDIENTS:

- 3 tbsp. salted butter
- 2 whole garlic cloves, crushed
- 1/2 cup onions, chopped
- 3 cups vegetable stock
- 16 oz. frozen broccoli florets
- 1 cup heavy whipping cream
- 2 cups sharp cheddar cheese, grated (extra for garnish)
- Himalayan salt
- Freshly ground black pepper

DIRECTIONS:

1. In a large pot over medium heat, melt the butter. When the butter is nice and hot, fry the garlic and onions for a few minutes, until the onions just begin to soften and lose their color.

2. Stir in the stock and broccoli florets, raise the heat to high, and stir until the stock begins to boil. Once the stock is boiling, lower the heat to maintain a gentle simmer for 15 minutes, until the broccoli is fork-tender, stirring at regular intervals to prevent burning.

3. With the heat on the lowest setting, add the cream and cheddar cheese to the pot, stirring until the cheese is melted and properly combined.

4. Taste the soup, and add salt and pepper to taste, if desired.

5. Ladle the soup into bowls, and serve hot, garnished with extra cheddar cheese.

Quick Tip:
Any leftovers can be refrigerated in an airtight container for no more than 5 days.

Per Serving:
Calories: 136, Fat: 8.8g, Protein: 2.1g, Carbohydrates: 9.4g, Fiber: 3.1g, Net Carbohydrates: 6.3g

TOMATO & HERB SOUP

COOK TIME: 35 MINS | MAKES: 4 SERVINGS

INGREDIENTS:

- 2 tbsp. salted butter
- 2 whole garlic cloves, crushed
- 1/2 cup onions, chopped
- 1/4 cup loosely packed fresh basil leaves (extra for garnish)
- 1 1/2 cups vegetable stock
- 28 oz. canned whole, peeled tomatoes
- 1/2 cup heavy whipping cream
- Himalayan salt
- Freshly ground black pepper
- Parmesan cheese, grated (for garnish)

DIRECTIONS:

1. In a medium-sized pot over medium heat, melt the butter. When the butter is nice and hot, fry the garlic and onions for a few minutes, until the onions start to lose their color and soften.

2. Stir in the basil leaves, vegetable stock, and peeled tomatoes. Raise the heat to high, and bring the soup to a boil. Once the soup begins to boil, lower the heat to maintain a gentle simmer for 2o minutes, stirring at regular intervals to prevent burning.

3. Transfer the pot to a wooden chopping board, and use a handheld immersion blender to purée the soup to the desired thickness.

4. Return the pot to the stove. With the heat on the lowest setting, stir in the cream, and simmer for an additional 15 minutes. Taste the soup, and season with salt and pepper to taste, if desired.

5. Ladle the soup into bowls, and serve hot, garnished with basil leaves and parmesan.

Quick Tip:
Any leftovers can be refrigerated in an airtight container for no more than 5 days.

Per Serving:
Calories: 205, Fat: 17.7g, Protein: 2.9g, Carbohydrates: 10.1g, Fiber: 4.2g, Net Carbohydrates: 5.9g

CREAMY CHICKEN CAULIFLOWER CHOWDER

COOK TIME: 25 MINS | MAKES: 6 SERVINGS

INGREDIENTS:

- 1/4 cup salted butter
- 1/2 medium onion, chopped
- 2 cups chicken stock
- 2 cups cauliflower florets, chopped
- 1/4 tsp. Himalayan salt
- 2 tsp. garlic powder
- 2 tbsp. dried minced onion
- 1 tbsp. dried parsley
- 3 oz. cream cheese
- 1 cup heavy whipping cream
- 1/2 cup cooked bacon, chopped
- 2 tsp. corn extract
- 1 1/2 lbs. cooked chicken, chopped

DIRECTIONS:

1. In a medium-sized pot over medium heat, melt the butter. When the butter is bubbling, fry the onions for a few minutes, until they just begin to caramelize.

2. Add the stock and cauliflower, and stir until the stock begins to simmer. Stir in the salt, garlic powder, dried minced onions, parsley, cream cheese, heavy whipping cream, and bacon, until all of the ingredients are properly incorporated into the soup.

3. Lower the heat to maintain a gentle simmer for 15-18 minutes, or until the chowder has thickened. Add the corn extract and cooked chicken, stirring for about 5 minutes, or until the chicken is hot.

4. Ladle the chowder into bowls, and serve hot.

Quick Tip:
Any leftovers can be refrigerated in an airtight container for no more than 5 days.

Per Serving:
Calories: 420, Fat: 26.6g, Protein: 36.3g, Carbohydrates: 3.1g, Fiber: 1.1g, Net Carbohydrates: 2g

SPICY TURMERIC & TURNIP SOUP

COOK TIME: 25 MINS | MAKES: 7 SERVINGS

INGREDIENTS:

- 1 tbsp. extra-virgin olive oil
- 1 tsp. crushed garlic
- 3 cups cauliflower florets
- 3 cups turnips, peeled and chopped
- 1 tsp. Himalayan salt
- 1/4 tsp. freshly ground black pepper
- 1 tsp. turmeric powder
- 1 tsp. onion powder
- 1 tsp. garam masala
- 1 tbsp. curry powder
- 4 cups chicken stock
- 1 cup canned coconut milk
- 1/4 cup fresh parsley, chopped (for garnish – optional)

DIRECTIONS:

1. In a large pot over medium heat, heat the olive oil. When the oil is nice and hot, fry the garlic, cauliflower, and turnips for about 5 minutes, or until the vegetables soften and begin to brown around the edges.

2. Stir in the salt, pepper, turmeric, onion powder, masala, curry powder, and chicken stock. When the stock begins to simmer, reduce the heat to maintain a gentle simmer for 20 minutes, or until the vegetables are soft.

3. When the vegetables are soft enough to be blended, add the coconut milk to the pot, and use an immersion blender to purée the soup until smooth.

4. Ladle the soup into bowls, and serve hot, garnished with fresh parsley, if desired.

Quick Tip:
Any leftover soup can be refrigerated in an airtight container for no more than 5 days, or frozen for no more than 3 months.

Per Serving:
Calories: 135, Fat: 9g, Protein: 3g, Carbohydrates: 9g, Fiber: 3g, Net Carbohydrates: 6g

ROASTED VEGETABLE SOUP

COOK TIME: 40 MINS | MAKES: 7 SERVINGS

INGREDIENTS:

- 1 garlic clove, peeled
- 1 cup leeks, washed and sliced
- 4 cups cauliflower florets
- 2 tbsp. extra-virgin avocado oil
- 2 tsp. Himalayan salt
- 1/4 tsp. freshly ground black pepper
- 1/8 tsp. ground nutmeg
- 1/4 tsp. dried thyme leaves
- 3 cups filtered water
- 3 cups beef stock
- 1 tsp. unsweetened balsamic vinegar
- 2 tbsp. unsalted butter
- 2 slices cooked bacon, chopped

DIRECTIONS:

1. Set the oven to preheat to 400°F, with the wire rack in the center of the oven.

2. Place the garlic, leeks, cauliflower, avocado oil, 1 teaspoon salt, and pepper on a large baking tray, and toss to coat. Place the tray in the oven for 25 minutes, or until the vegetables soften and crisp up around the edges with a lovely golden brown.

3. Scrape the roasted vegetables into a large pot, along with the nutmeg, thyme, filtered water, and stock. Bring the soup to a gentle boil over medium heat, stirring at regular intervals for 15 minutes. The vegetables should be soft enough to blend.

4. Add the butter, remaining salt, and vinegar to the pot. Use an immersion blender to purée the soup until smooth.

5. Ladle the soup into bowls, and garnish with bacon bits before serving hot.

Quick Tip:
Any leftovers can be refrigerated in an airtight container for no more than 5 days, or frozen for no more than 3 months.

Per Serving:
Calories: 142, Fat: 10g, Protein: 4g, Carbohydrates: 6g, Fiber: 2g, Net Carbohydrates: 4g

CHORIZO & SPINACH SOUP

COOK TIME: 28 MINS | MAKES: 12 SERVINGS

INGREDIENTS:

- 1 tbsp. extra-virgin olive oil
- 1 lb. chorizo sausage, casings removed, sliced
- 2 garlic cloves, minced
- 1/2 cup onions, chopped
- 1 tsp. Himalayan salt
- 1/4 tsp. freshly ground black pepper
- 1/4 tsp. cayenne pepper
- 4 cups filtered water
- 4 cups chicken stock
- 2 cups zucchini, roughly chopped
- 3 cups spinach, chopped

DIRECTIONS:

1. In a large pot over medium heat, heat the olive oil. When the oil is nice and hot, fry the chorizo for 5 minutes, breaking the meat apart as it cooks.

2. Stir in the garlic and onions for 3 minutes, allowing the flavors to meld, until the onions soften and start to lose their color.

3. Stir in the salt, pepper, cayenne pepper, filtered water, chicken stock, zucchini, and spinach. Bring the soup to a gentle simmer, and maintain for 20 minutes, stirring at regular intervals until the chorizo is cooked all the way through, and the vegetables have softened.

4. Ladle the soup into bowls, and serve hot.

Quick Tip:
Any leftovers can be refrigerated in an airtight container for no more than 5 days, or frozen for no more than 3 months.

Per Serving:
Calories: 186, Fat: 14g, Protein: 11g, Carbohydrates: 6g, Fiber: 1g, Net Carbohydrates: 5g

CHEESY CAULIFLOWER & BACON SOUP

COOK TIME: 20 MINS | MAKES: 4 SERVINGS

INGREDIENTS:

- 3 tbsp. salted butter
- 2 garlic cloves, minced
- 1/2 cup onions, chopped
- 2 cups vegetable stock
- 16 oz. frozen cauliflower florets
- 1 cup heavy whipping cream
- 2 cups sharp cheddar cheese, grated (extra for garnish)
- Himalayan salt
- Freshly ground black pepper
- 8 slices cooked bacon, roughly chopped

DIRECTIONS:

1. In a medium-sized pot over medium heat, melt the butter. When the butter is hot and bubbling, fry the garlic and onions for a few minutes, until the onions begin to soften and lose their color.

2. Stir in the stock and cauliflower florets. Raise the heat, and stir until the soup begins to boil. Once the soup is boiling, lower the heat to maintain a gentle simmer for 15 minutes, or until the cauliflower is tender. Stir the pot at regular intervals to prevent burning.

3. With the heat on the lowest setting, stir in the cream and cheese, until the cheese is completely melted and incorporated into the soup.

4. Taste the soup, and season with salt and pepper, as desired.

5. Ladle the soup into bowls, and garnish with extra cheddar and bacon before serving hot.

Quick Tip:
Any leftovers can be refrigerated in an airtight container for no more than 5 days.

Per Serving:
Calories: 186, Fat: 14g, Protein: 11g, Carbohydrates: 6g, Fiber: 1g, Net Carbohydrates: 5g

SPICY BEEF & CHEESE SOUP

COOK TIME: 1 HOUR 15 MINS | MAKES: 8 SERVINGS

INGREDIENTS:

- 1 tsp. extra-virgin olive oil
- 2 garlic cloves, minced
- 1/2 cup onions, diced
- 2 lbs. ground beef
- 8 oz. cream cheese
- 1 tsp. cayenne pepper
- 2 tbsp. ground cumin
- 4 cups vegetable stock
- 4 oz. canned green chilies, diced
- 15 oz. canned tomato sauce
- 14 1/2 oz. canned petite diced tomatoes
- Himalayan salt
- Freshly ground black pepper
- Fresh coriander leaves, chopped (for garnish)
- Avocado, sliced (for garnish)
- Sharp cheddar cheese, grated (for garnish)
- Sour cream (for garnish)

DIRECTIONS:

1. In a large pot over medium heat, heat the olive oil. When the oil is nice and hot, fry the garlic, onions, and ground beef for about 10 minutes, or until the ground beef is nicely browned. Strain off any excess fat and oil.

2. Stir in the cream cheese for a few minutes, until completely incorporated into the beef.

3. Add the cayenne pepper, cumin, stock, green chilies, tomato sauce, and diced petite tomatoes. Bring the soup to a boil while stirring. Once the soup begins to boil, lower the heat to maintain a gentle simmer for 1 hour, allowing the flavors to meld. Stir the pot at regular intervals, and keep an eye on the heat to prevent burning. The soup should not boil.

4. Taste the soup, and season with salt and pepper as desired.

5. Ladle the hot soup into bowls, and serve with your choice of garnish.

Per Serving:
Calories: 405, Fat: 29.2g, Protein: 23.8g, Carbohydrates: 9.1g, Fiber: 2.5g, Net Carbohydrates: 6.6g

HEARTY BEEF SOUP

COOK TIME: 40 MINS | MAKES: 6 SERVINGS

INGREDIENTS:

- 2 tbsp. salted butter
- 1 garlic clove, minced
- 1/4 cup onions, diced
- 1/2 cup celery, diced
- 1 lb. ground beef
- 1 tsp. dried parsley
- 1 tsp. dried basil
- 12 oz. frozen cauliflower florets
- 3 cups vegetable stock
- 1 cup heavy whipping cream
- 2 cups sharp cheddar cheese, shredded
- Himalayan salt
- Freshly ground black pepper

DIRECTIONS:

1. In a large pot over medium heat, melt the butter. When the butter is bubbling, fry the garlic, onions, and celery for a few minutes, until the onions lose their color and the celery softens.

2. Stir in the ground beef, and cook until nicely browned, separating the meat with a wooden spoon as it cooks. Discard any excess fat and oil from the pot.

3. Stir in the parsley, basil, cauliflower, and stock. Bring the soup to a boil, before lowering the heat to maintain a gentle simmer for 25 minutes. Stir the soup at regular intervals to prevent burning.

4. With the heat on the lowest setting, stir in the cream and cheese until the cheese is completely incorporated into the soup.

5. Taste the soup, and season with salt and pepper as desired. Ladle the soup into bowls, and serve hot.

Quick Tip:
Any leftovers can be refrigerated in an airtight container for no more than 5 days.

Per Serving:
Calories: 544, Fat: 46.9g, Protein: 23.8g, Carbohydrates: 6.1g, Fiber: 1.7g, Net Carbohydrates: 4.4g

DESSERTS

CHOCOLATE PEANUT BUTTER BITES

COOK TIME: 16 MINS | MAKES: 12 SERVINGS

INGREDIENTS:

- 5 drops liquid stevia
- 1/2 tsp. pure vanilla essence
- 1 tsp. baking powder
- 1/2 cup granular erythritol
- 1/2 cup sugar-free chocolate chips
- 2 large free-range eggs
- 1 cup natural peanut butter (any texture)

DIRECTIONS:

1. Grease a large baking pan, and set the oven to preheat to 375°F, with the wire rack in the center of the oven.

2. In a large mixing bowl, use a wooden spoon to combine the stevia, vanilla, baking powder, erythritol, chocolate chips, eggs, and peanut butter. Scrape the mixture into the greased baking pan in an even layer.

3. Place the pan in the oven for 14-16 minutes. Keep an eye on the oven as the bites bake; this recipe can burn quite quickly. Take the pan out of the oven when the center is set and the edges are nicely browned.

4. Allow the pan to cool completely on the counter, before slicing into 12 bites, and serving.

Quick Tip:
Any leftovers can be stored in an airtight container for no more than 1 week.

Per Serving:
Calories: 146, Fat: 12.3g, Protein: 6.3g, Carbohydrates: 7.1g, Fiber: 2.8g, Net Carbohydrates: 4.3g

STRAWBERRIES & CREAM KETO PIE

COOK TIME: 0 MINS | MAKES: 8 SERVINGS

INGREDIENTS:

- 1/4 tsp. Himalayan salt
- 1 tbsp. unsalted butter, melted
- 3 tbsp. granulated sweetener
- 3/4 cup blanched almond flour
- 8 oz. cream cheese, at room temperature
- 2 tsp. pure vanilla essence
- 1 tsp. strawberry essence
- 2 tbsp. freshly squeezed lemon juice
- 1/2 cup powdered sweetener
- 1 1/4 cups heavy whipping cream
- 1 cup fresh strawberries, thinly sliced (extra for garnish)

DIRECTIONS:

1. In a high-powered food processor, pulse the salt, butter, granulated sweetener, and flour a few times, until the mixture resembles fine sand. Scrape the mixture into a large baking dish, and use the bottom of a clean glass to press it into a crust.

2. Place the cream cheese in a large mixing bowl, and use a handheld mixer to beat the it into a smooth paste. Once the cream cheese is smooth, beat in the vanilla, strawberry essence, lemon juice, and powdered sweetener, until the ingredients are properly incorporated.

3. Add the cream in 3 batches, beating the mixture with a handheld beater after every addition. Fold in the sliced strawberries once the mixture is light and fluffy. Scrape the filling onto the crust in the prepared baking dish, using an offset spatula to smooth out the top.

4. Garnish the top of the pie with extra fresh strawberries if desired, and refrigerate for a minimum of 4 hours, or overnight.

5. Slice and serve the chilled pie.

Per Serving:
Calories: 320, Fat: 31.9g, Protein: 3.9g, Carbohydrates: 4.8g, Fiber: 1.9g, Net Carbohydrates: 2.9g

NO-FUSS PECAN COOKIES

COOK TIME: 1 HOUR | MAKES: 18 SERVINGS

INGREDIENTS:

- 1/8 tsp. Himalayan salt
- 1/8 tsp. cream of tartar
- Whites of 2 large free-range eggs, at room temperature
- 2 tbsp. powdered sweetener
- 1 tsp. pure vanilla essence
- 1 tbsp. chopped dark chocolate (90% cocoa)
- 2 tbsp. pecans, roughly chopped

DIRECTIONS:

1. Cover a large, rimmed baking tray with greaseproof paper. Generously grease the paper. Set the oven to preheat to 225°F, with the wire rack in the center of the oven.

2. Place the salt, cream of tartar, and egg whites in a large bowl, and use a handheld mixer to beat the egg whites until frothy. Gradually pour the sweetener in while beating the egg whites on the lowest setting. Add the vanilla essence, and beat until the egg whites resemble fluffy clouds with stiff peaks. Fold in the dark chocolate and chopped pecans using an offset spatula.

3. Gently drop the batter onto the prepared baking tray, using about 1 tablespoon of batter per cookie, and spacing them about 1-inch apart. Bake the cookies in the oven for 1 hour. When they are lightly toasted, turn off the heat, and leave the tray in the oven overnight with the door closed.

4. Serve the cookies the next day, and enjoy!

Per Serving:
Calories: 8, Fat: 0g, Protein: 1.2g, Carbohydrates: 0.2g, Fiber: 0g, Net Carbohydrates: 0.2g

NUTTY-CRUSTED KETO CHEESECAKE

COOK TIME: 1 HOUR 45 MINS | MAKES: 16 SERVINGS

INGREDIENTS:

- 1/4 cup salted butter
- 1/2 cup granular erythritol
- 1 cup raw pecans, roughly chopped
- 1 cup ground blanched almond flour
- 1/4 tsp. ground nutmeg
- 8 oz. cream cheese, at room temperature
- 1 1/2 cups confectioners'-style erythritol
- 4 large free-range eggs
- 1 cup sour cream
- 1 tsp. pure vanilla essence
- 1 tbsp. freshly squeezed lemon juice

DIRECTIONS:

1. Generously grease a large springform pan with butter, and set the oven to preheat to 375°F, with the wire rack in the center of the oven.

2. In a large mixing bowl, combine the butter, granular erythritol, pecans, almond flour, and nutmeg, until you have a crumbly mixture. Scrape the mixture into the prepared baking pan, and use the bottom of a clean glass to press it into a crust. Bake the crust in the oven for 12-15 minutes, or until the edges are nicely browned. Remove the pan from the oven, and allow the crust to cool completely on the counter. Reduce the oven to 325°F while the crust cools.

3. When the crust is completely cool, place the cream cheese in a large mixing bowl, and beat with a handheld mixer until smooth.

4. When the cream cheese is fluffy, beat in the confectioner's-style erythritol on medium. When the erythritol is properly incorporated, beat in the eggs, 1 at a time, using a wooden spoon or offset spatula to scrape down the sides of the bowl as you go.

5. Beat in the sour cream, then add the vanilla and lemon juice, and beat until you have a thick, lump-free batter.

6. Cover the bottom of the pan with the cooled crust in aluminum foil, to protect the cake from the water bath.

7. Scrape the cream cheese filling into the crust, and use an offset spatula to smooth out the top. Place the pan in a baking dish, and fill the dish with boiling water that comes to about halfway up the pan.

8. Place the pan, along with the water bath, in the oven for 1 hour and 30 minutes, or until the center of the cheesecake is no longer runny, and the top is lightly toasted.

9. Allow the cheesecake to cool completely on the counter, before chilling for a minimum of 8 hours or overnight.

10. Once the cake is nicely chilled, run a warm knife around the edge of the springform pan to loosen the cake. Remove the pan, slice the cake, and serve.

Per Serving:
Calories: 315, Fat: 28.1g, Protein: 8.7g, Carbohydrates: 3.6g, Net Carbohydrates: 2.3g

FRUITY KETO DESSERT PIZZA

COOK TIME: 14 MINS | MAKES: 8 SERVINGS

INGREDIENTS:

- 1 tsp. baking powder
- 1/3 cup granular erythritol
- 1 1/4 cups blanched almond flour
- 1 large free-range egg
- 1 tsp. pure vanilla essence
- 5 tbsp. salted butter, at room temperature
- 1 tbsp. heavy whipping cream
- 2 tbsp. confectioners'-style erythritol
- 5 oz. cream cheese, softened
- 1/2 cup fresh blueberries
- 1/2 cup whole raspberries

DIRECTIONS:

1. Set the oven to preheat to 350°F, with the wire rack in the center of the oven, and generously grease the bottom of a large springform pan.

2. In a medium-sized mixing bowl, whisk together the baking powder, granular erythritol, and almond flour. Set aside.

3. In a separate mixing bowl, beat the egg before adding in the vanilla and butter. Beat the mixture until everything is properly combined. Scrape the egg mixture into the bowl of flour, and beat until you have a smooth batter. Scrape the batter into the prepared pan in an even layer, and bake in the oven for 12-14 minutes, or until the crust is golden around the edges. Allow the crust to cool completely in the pan before removing.

4. Meanwhile, in a small mixing bowl, whisk the cream, confectioners'-style erythritol, and cream cheese, until you have a smooth mixture. Spoon the mixture onto the cooled crust in an even layer, and top with the berries.

5. Close the pizza in cling wrap, and chill for 2 hours before slicing and serving.

Per Serving:
Calories: 230, Fat: 20.4g, Protein: 5.6g, Carbohydrates: 5.2g, Net Carbohydrates: 3.1g

TWO-MINUTE BLACKBERRY COBBLER

COOK TIME: 2 MINS | MAKES: 2 SERVINGS

INGREDIENTS:

- 1/4 tsp. pure vanilla essence
- 1/4 tsp. keto-friendly sweetener
- 1 1/2 cups fresh blackberries
- 1/2 tsp. baking powder
- 1/4 cup fine blanched almond flour
- 1/4 tsp. ground nutmeg
- 1/4 cup cold salted butter, cut into small cubes
- Optional whipped cream for serving

DIRECTIONS:

1. Grease a small, microwave-safe baking dish with butter.

2. Place the vanilla, sweetener, and blackberries in a small bowl, and use a wooden spoon to gently fold the mixture together. Scrape the berry mixture into the buttered dish in an even layer.

3. In a clean mixing bowl, mix together the baking powder, almond flour, and nutmeg. Add the butter, and use pastry knives to cut the butter cubes into the flour mixture, until it resembles bread crumbs. Sprinkle the mixture over the blackberries in the baking dish.

4. Place the dish in the microwave for 1 1/2-2 minutes, until the topping is lightly toasted, and the berry mixture is bubbling. Check the dish every 30 seconds, as cooking time may vary, depending on the microwave strength.

5. Allow the cobbler to stand on the counter for 10 minutes, before serving with optional whipped cream.

Quick Tip:
You may want to taste the sweetness of the berries before adding the sweetener, and adjust the amount according to taste.

Per Serving:
Calories: 328, Fat: 30g, Protein: 4.3g, Carbohydrates: 12.8g, Fiber: 7g, Net Carbohydrates: 5.8g

QUICK & EASY BOURBON BALLS

COOK TIME: 3 MINS | MAKES: 12 SERVINGS

INGREDIENTS:

- 1 cup confectioners'-style erythritol
- 1/2 cup salted butter, softened
- 1/2 tsp. pure vanilla essence
- 3 tbsp. Maker's Mark bourbon
- 1/4 cup raw pecans, roughly chopped
- 1 tbsp. coconut oil
- 3/4 cup sugar-free chocolate chips
- 12 raw pecan halves (for garnish)

DIRECTIONS:

1. In a large mixing bowl, beat the erythritol and butter until the mixture is light and fluffy. Beat in the vanilla and bourbon, before gently folding in the chopped pecans. Cover the bowl in cling wrap, and chill for 3o minutes.

2. In a small glass bowl, microwave the coconut oil and chocolate chips for 1-2 minutes, or until the chocolate is properly incorporated into the oil. Stir the chocolate and coconut oil every 30 seconds, until you have a lump-free mixture.

3. Once the batter has chilled, use clean hands to roll the batter into 12 balls of roughly the same size. Arrange the balls on an aluminum-foil-lined baking tray. Dip each ball in the melted chocolate before returning to the tray. Garnish each coated ball with 1 pecan half.

4. Chill the balls for 1 hour, then allow them to stand on the counter for 10 minutes before serving.

Per Serving:
Calories: 117, Fat: 11.5g, Protein: 0.8g, Carbohydrates: 4.8g, Fiber: 3.8g, Net Carbohydrates: 1g

COCONUTTY CHOCOLATE BOMBS

COOK TIME: 0 MINS | MAKES: 8 SERVINGS

INGREDIENTS:

- 1 tsp. coconut oil
- 1 cup sugar-free chocolate chips
- 1/4 cup salted butter
- 1 cup unsweetened shredded coconut (extra for garnish)

DIRECTIONS:

1. Place the coconut oil and chocolate chips in a small glass bowl, and microwave on high for 30-second intervals, stirring in-between, until the chocolate has melted.

2. Add the butter, and stir with a fork until combined.

3. Stir in the shredded coconut.

4. Spoon the mixture into 8 cups of a rubber cupcake mold, and garnish with extra shredded coconut. Place the rubber mold on a baking tray, and freeze for 2 hours. Unmold and serve.

Per Serving:
Calories: 165, Fat: 13.9g, Protein: 3.9g, Carbohydrates: 4.4g, Fiber: 3g, Net Carbohydrates: 1.4g

KETO-STYLE COCONUT BUNDT CAKE

COOK TIME: 55 MINS | MAKES: 10 SERVINGS

INGREDIENTS:

- 1/2 tsp. Himalayan salt
- 2 tsp. baking powder
- 3/4 cup granular erythritol
- 1/4 cup coconut flour
- 2 cups finely ground almond flour
- 2 1/2 tsp. pure vanilla, essence (divided)
- 1/4 cup pure coconut oil, melted
- 1/2 cup salted butter, at room temperature
- 5 large free-range eggs
- 1 1/2 cups unsweetened shredded coconut (divided)
- 1/4 cup heavy whipping cream
- 1/2 cup confectioners'-style erythritol

DIRECTIONS:

1. Grease a large Bundt mold with butter, and set the oven to preheat to 350°F, with the wire rack in the center of the oven.

2. In a medium-sized mixing bowl, mix together the salt, baking powder, granular erythritol, coconut flour, and almond flour. Set aside. In a large mixing bowl, beat together 2 teaspoons of vanilla, the coconut oil, butter, and eggs until properly combined.

3. With the mixer on the lowest setting, gradually add the flour mixture to the wet ingredients, and beat until you have a lump-free batter. Gently fold in 1 cup shredded coconut with a wooden spoon.

4. Scrape the batter into the greased mold, and use an offset spatula to smooth out the top. Bake the cake in the oven for 45 minutes, or until an inserted skewer comes out clean. Allow the cake to cool on the counter, and reduce the oven temperature to 325°F.

5. Line a large, rimmed baking sheet with greaseproof paper. Spread the remaining 1/2 cup of shredded coconut over the paper in a single layer. Place the sheet in the oven for 10 minutes, gently tossing and stirring the flakes half way through. Keep an eye on the coconut, and remove the sheet as soon as the flakes start turning brown. Allow the coconut to cool on the counter.

6. In a small glass bowl, whisk 1/2 teaspoon vanilla with the cream and confectioners' erythritol, until you have a lump-free glaze.

7. When the cake is completely cooled, place a plate under the mold, and gently flip the cake before removing the mold. Pour the glaze over the cake, and garnish with the toasted coconut before serving.

Per Serving:
Calories: 361, Fat: 31.4g, Protein: 10.2g, Carbohydrates: 7.5g, Fiber: 5.4g, Net Carbohydrates: 3.1g

LIME & COCONUT CHEESECAKE BALLS

COOK TIME: 0 MINS | MAKES: 12 SERVINGS

INGREDIENTS:

- 8 drops keto-friendly liquid sweetener
- 2 tsp. freshly squeezed lime juice
- 2 tsp. grated lime zest
- 6 tbsp. cream cheese, at room temperature
- 2/3 cup coconut oil, melted
- 1 drop almond extract
- 7 tbsp. unsweetened shredded coconut

DIRECTIONS:

1. Cover a large, rimmed baking sheet with greaseproof paper.

2. In a medium-sized mixing bowl, whisk together the sweetener, lime juice, lime zest, cream cheese, coconut oil, almond extract, and 4 tablespoons of shredded coconut.

3. Use a tablespoon to gently drop the mixture onto the prepared baking sheet, in 12 evenly spaced portions.

4. Chill the sheet for 1-2 hours, or until the portions have begun to harden, but aren't quite hard yet.

5. Use clean hands to roll the 12 portions into balls, and dip them in the remaining coconut before returning them to the sheet.

6. Serve, and enjoy.

Quick Tip:
Any leftovers can be refrigerated in an airtight container for no more than 1 week.

Per Serving:
Calories: 155, Fat: 16g, Protein: 1g, Carbohydrates: 2g, Fiber: 1g, Net Carbohydrates: 1g

CHOCOLATE TRUFFLE BOMBS

COOK TIME: 0 MINS | MAKES: 12 SERVINGS

INGREDIENTS:

- 1/4 cup coconut oil
- 1 tsp. instant espresso powder
- 1/4 cup unsweetened cocoa powder
- 12 drops keto-friendly liquid sweetener
- 2 oz. cream cheese, softened
- 1/2 cup almond butter

DIRECTIONS:

1. Cover a large, rimmed baking sheet with greaseproof paper.

2. In a medium-sized glass bowl, microwave the coconut oil on high, until completely melted, stirring with a fork at regular intervals. When the coconut oil has melted, whisk in the espresso powder and cocoa powder until properly incorporated. Add the sweetener, cream cheese, and almond butter, and whisk until you have a lump-free mixture.

3. Use a tablespoon to drop the mixture onto the prepared baking sheet in 12 evenly spaced portions.

4. Chill the sheet for 3o minutes, until the bombs are firm to the touch. Serve and enjoy.

Per Serving:
Calories: 125, Fat: 12g, Protein: 3g, Carbohydrates: 4g, Fiber: 1g, Net Carbohydrates: 3g

RASPBERRY KETO PRESERVE

COOK TIME: 2-3 MINS | MAKES: 2-4 SERVINGS

INGREDIENTS:

- 3 cups fresh raspberries
- 3 tbsp. filtered water
- 2 tsp. sugar-free vanilla essence
- 15 drops liquid stevia
- 3 tbsp. chia seeds

DIRECTIONS:

1. Place the raspberries in a high-powered food processor, and pulse on high until you have a smooth jam.

2. Scrape the raspberry jam into a small pot, along with the filtered water. Bring the mixture to a boil over medium heat, while stirring for 2-3 minutes. Transfer the pot to a wooden chopping board, and stir in the vanilla and stevia. Add the chia seeds, and stir to combine.

3. Let the preserve rest on the counter for 20 minutes; it will thicken as it cools.

4. Scoop the preserve into a jar, and use immediately or chill.

Quick Tip:
The preserve can be chilled in a sealed jar for no more than 1 week, or frozen in an ice cube tray for no more than 6 months.

Per Serving:
Calories: 29, Fat: 0.9g, Protein: 0.8g, Carbohydrates: 4.9g, Fiber: 2.9g, Net Carbohydrates: 2g

BERRY-STUDDED LEMON MOUSSE

COOK TIME: 10 MINS | MAKES: 5 SERVINGS

INGREDIENTS:

- 4 large free-range eggs
- 1/3 cup confectioners'-style erythritol
- 1 tbsp. finely grated lemon zest
- 1/2 cup freshly squeezed lemon juice
- 1 cup heavy whipping cream
- 1 1/2 cups fresh blackberries

DIRECTIONS:

1. Crack 2 eggs into a large glass mixing bowl along with the yolks of the other 2. Place the 2 separate egg whites in another bowl, and set aside. Lightly whisk the bowl of whole eggs and yolks, before whisking in the erythritol, lemon zest, and lemon juice.

2. Place the bowl over a pot of boiling water; the water should not be touching the bottom of the bowl. Continuously whisk the mixture for 10 minutes, until it has thickened. Transfer the bowl to a wooden chopping board, and let stand for 5 minutes.

3. Meanwhile, beat the egg whites until stiff peaks form. In a separate bowl, beat the cream until thick. Gently fold the egg whites into the bowl with the cooled mixture. Once the egg whites are properly incorporated, fold in the cream.

4. Place a few blackberries in the bottom of 5 serving bowls and top with the mousse. Garnish each bowl with more blackberries, and serve.

Per Serving:
Calories: 256, Fat: 22.3g, Protein: 6.5g, Carbohydrates: 7.4g, Fiber: 2.1g, Net Carbohydrates: 5.3g

ONE-PAN BERRY CRUMBLE

COOK TIME: 15 MINS | MAKES: 6 SERVINGS

INGREDIENTS:

- 1 tbsp. pure coconut oil
- 1 cup fresh blueberries
- 1 cup fresh raspberries
- 5-10 drops keto-friendly liquid sweetener (optional)
- 2 tbsp. granulated erythritol
- 1/4 tsp. Himalayan salt
- 1 tsp. ground cinnamon
- 1/4 tsp. ground nutmeg
- 2 tbsp. unsalted butter
- 1/2 cup raw pecans
- 1 cup raw almonds
- Plain Greek yogurt (for topping)
- Sour cream (for topping)
- Mascarpone cheese (for topping)
- Coconut milk flavored with vanilla essence (for topping)

DIRECTIONS:

1. Set the oven to preheat to 400°F, with the wire rack in the center of the oven.

2. In a large, oven-safe frying pan over medium-high heat, melt the coconut oil. When the coconut oil has melted, stir in the berries for 3-5 minutes, or until they have softened. Taste the berry mixture, and add sweetener to taste if desired. Transfer the pan to a wooden chopping board.

3. Preheat the oven broiler.

4. Place the granulated erythritol, salt, cinnamon, nutmeg, butter, pecans, and almonds in a high-powered food processor, and pulse on high until the mixture resembles coarse sand.

5. Sprinkle the mixture over the berries in the pan in an even layer.

6. Place the pan in the oven for 10 minutes, or until the crumble is lightly toasted.

7. Allow the pan to cool for 5 minutes on the counter, before serving the crumble with a topping of your choice.

Per Serving:
Calories: 275, Fat: 24.8g, Protein: 6.4g, Carbohydrates: 10.8g, Fiber: 5.3g, Net Carbohydrates: 5.5g

CHOCOLATE CHIP PUMPKIN COOKIES

COOK TIME: 13-15 MINS | MAKES: 12 SERVINGS

INGREDIENTS:

- 1/4 tsp. Himalayan salt
- 5-10 drops keto-friendly liquid sweetener
- 2 tbsp. granulated erythritol
- 1 tbsp. pumpkin pie spice mix
- 1/3 cup no-sugar-added pumpkin purée
- 1 large free-range egg
- 1 cup almond butter
- 1/2 tsp. pure vanilla essence
- 1/2 cup dark chocolate chips

DIRECTIONS:

1. Set the oven to preheat to 350°F, with the wire rack in the center of the oven.

2. In a high-powered food processor, pulse the salt, optional sweetener, erythritol, pumpkin pie spice, pumpkin purée, egg, almond butter, and vanilla until you have a lump-free batter. Scrape the batter into a mixing bowl, and fold in the chocolate chips with a wooden spoon.

3. Use an ice cream scoop to portion the cookies into 10 balls. Place the balls on a greaseproof-paper-lined baking sheet, and use a fork to gently flatten them into cookies.

4. Bake the cookies in the oven for 13-15 minutes, or until they are golden brown and crisp around the edges. Transfer the cookies to a wire cooling rack, and cool completely before serving.

Quick Tip:
These cookies can be refrigerated in an airtight container for no more than 1 week, or frozen for no more than 3 months.

Per Serving:
Calories: 224, Fat: 17.1g, Protein: 6.4g, Carbohydrates: 8.4g, Fiber: 4.4, Net Carbohydrates: 4g

Made in United States
North Haven, CT
28 August 2022